Marx Abbott Hardy Montaigne Machiavelli Chesterton Cooper Emerson Joyce Austen Defoe Melville Haggard Hugo Eliot Grimm Carroll Christie Stoker Molière Wilde Byron Maupassant Schiller Engels Einstein Fitzgerald Garnett Smith Hawthorne Kafka Goethe Dostoyevsky Hall Cotton Kipling Doyle Baum Willis Leslie Dumas Henry Nietzsche Flaubert Turgenev Balzac Stockton Vatsyayana Crane Burroughs Verne Whitman Gogol Vinci Curtis Tocqueville Homer Widger Tolstoy Busch Darwin Thoreau Potter Freud Zola Twain Plato Scott Lawrence Kant Jowett Stevenson Dickens Andersen Burton Hesse Harte Cervantes London Descartes Voltaire Poe Aristotle Wells Hale James Hastings Cooke Bunner Shakespeare Richter Chambers Irving da Chekhov Benedict Doré Swift Dante Shaw Wodehouse Alcott Pushkin Newton tredition®

tredition was established in 2006 by Sandra Latusseck and Soenke Schulz. Based in Hamburg, Germany, tredition offers publishing solutions to authors and publishing houses, combined with worldwide distribution of printed and digital book content. tredition is uniquely positioned to enable authors and publishing houses to create books on their own terms and without conventional manufacturing risks.

For more information please visit: www.tredition.com

TREDITION CLASSICS

This book is part of the TREDITION CLASSICS series. The creators of this series are united by passion for literature and driven by the intention of making all public domain books available in printed format again - worldwide. Most TREDITION CLASSICS titles have been out of print and off the bookstore shelves for decades. At tredition we believe that a great book never goes out of style and that its value is eternal. Several mostly non-profit literature projects provide content to tredition. To support their good work, tredition donates a portion of the proceeds from each sold copy. As a reader of a TREDITION CLASSICS book, you support our mission to save many of the amazing works of world literature from oblivion. See all available books at www.tredition.com.

Project Gutenberg

The content for this book has been graciously provided by Project Gutenberg. Project Gutenberg is a non-profit organization founded by Michael Hart in 1971 at the University of Illinois. The mission of Project Gutenberg is simple: To encourage the creation and distribution of eBooks. Project Gutenberg is the first and largest collection of public domain eBooks.

A Color Notation A measured color system, based on the three qualities Hue, Value and Chroma

A. H. (Albert Henry) Munsell

Imprint

This book is part of TREDITION CLASSICS

Author: A. H. (Albert Henry) Munsell
Cover design: Buchgut, Berlin – Germany

Publisher: tredition GmbH, Hamburg - Germany
ISBN: 978-3-8472-1623-0

www.tredition.com
www.tredition.de

The intention of the TREDITION CLASSICS series is to make world literature in the public domain available in printed format. Literary enthusiasts and organizations, such as Project Gutenberg, worldwide have scanned and digitally edited the original texts. tredition has subsequently formatted and redesigned the content into a modern reading layout. Therefore, we cannot guarantee the exact reproduction of the original format of a particular historic edition. Please also note that no modifications have been made to the spelling, therefore it may differ from the orthography used today.

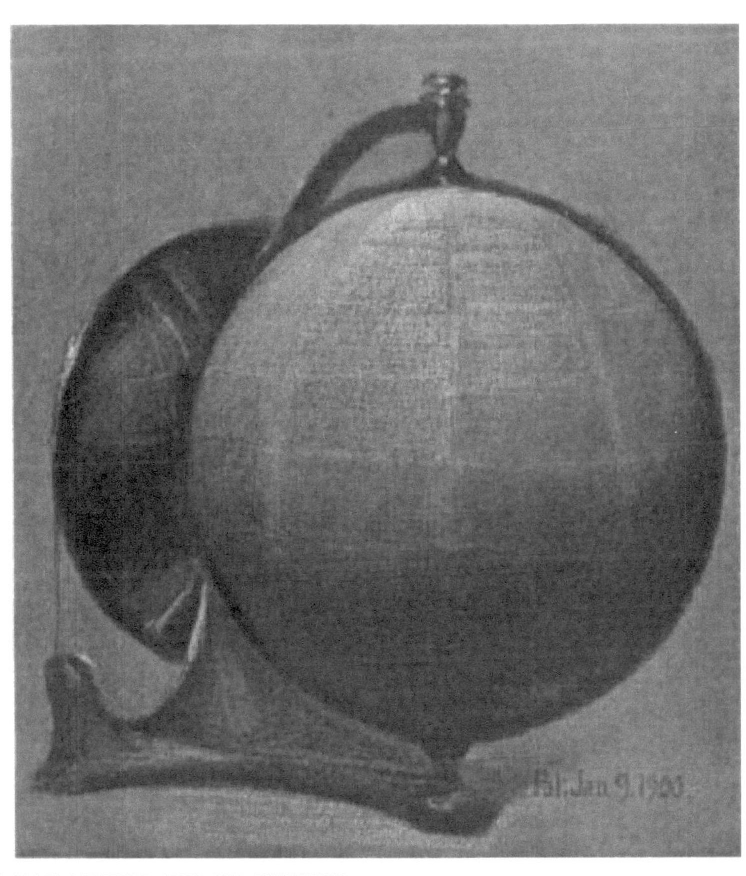

A BALANCED COLOR SPHERE
PASTEL SKETCH

A COLOR NOTATION

By

A. H. MUNSELL

A MEASURED COLOR
SYSTEM, BASED ON THE
THREE QUALITIES
Hue, Value, and Chroma

WITH

ILLUSTRATIVE MODELS, CHARTS,
AND A COURSE OF STUDY
ARRANGED FOR TEACHERS

2nd Edition
Revised &
Enlarged

GEO. H. ELLIS CO.
BOSTON
1907

3

AUTHOR'S PREFACE.

At various times during the past ten years, the gist of these pages has been given in the form of lectures to students of the Normal Art School, the Art Teachers' Association, and the Twentieth Century Club. In October of last year it was presented before the Society of Arts of the Massachusetts Institute of Technology, at the suggestion of Professor Charles R. Cross.

Grateful acknowledgment is due to many whose helpful criticism has aided in its development, notably Mr. Benjamin Ives Gilman, Secretary of the Museum of Fine Arts, Professor Harry E. Clifford, of the Institute, and Mr. Myron T. Pritchard, master of the Everett School, Boston.

A. H. M.

CHESTNUT HILL, MASS., 1905.

PREFACE TO SECOND EDITION.

The new illustrations in this edition are facsimiles of children's studies with measured color, made under ordinary school-room conditions. Notes and appendices are introduced to meet the questions most frequently asked, stress being laid on the unbalanced nature of colors usually given to beginners, and the mischief done by teaching that red, yellow, and blue are primary hues.

The need of a scientific basis for color values is also emphasized, believing this to be essential in the discipline of the color sense.

A. H. M.

Chestnut Hill, Mass., 1907.

INTRODUCTION.

The lack of definiteness which is at present so general in color nomenclature, is due in large measure to the failure to appreciate the fundamental characteristics on which color differences depend. For the physicist, the expression of the wave length of any particular light is in most cases sufficient, but in the great majority of instances where colors are referred to, something more than this and something easier of realization is essential.

The attempt to express color relations by using merely two dimensions, or two definite characteristics, can never lead to a successful system. For this reason alone the system proposed by Mr. Munsell, with its three dimensions of hue, value, and chroma, is a decided step in advance over any previous proposition. By means of these three dimensions it is possible to completely express any particular color, and to differentiate it from colors ordinarily classed as of the same general character.

The expression of the essential characteristics of a color is, however, not all that is necessary. There must be some accurate and not too complicated system for duplicating these characteristics, one which shall not alter with time or place, and which shall be susceptible of easy and accurate redetermination. From the teaching standpoint also a logical and sequential development is absolutely essential. This Mr. Munsell seems to have most successfully accomplished.

5

In the determination of his relationships he has made use of distinctly scientific methods, and there seems no reason why his suggestions should not lead to an exact and definite system of color essentials. The Munsell photometer, which is briefly referred to, is an instrument of wide range, high precision, and great sensitiveness, and permits the valuations which are necessary in his system to be accurately made. We all appreciate the necessity for some improvement in our ideas of color, and the natural inference is that the training should be begun in early youth. The present system in its modified form possesses elements of simplicity and attractiveness which should appeal to children, and give them almost unconsciously a power of discrimination which would prove of immense value in later life. The possibilities in this system are very great, and it has been a privilege to be allowed during the past few years to keep in touch with its development. Icannot but feel that we have here not only a rational color nomenclature, but also a system of scientific importance and of practical value.

H. E. Clifford.

MASSACHUSETTS INSTITUTE OF TECHNOLOGY,
February, 1905.
7

Chapter I.
COLOR NAMES.

Writing from Samoa to Sidney Colvin in London, Stevenson1 says: "Perhaps in the same way it might amuse you to send us any pattern of wall paper that might strike you as cheap, pretty, and suitable for a room in a hot and extremely bright climate. It should be borne in mind that our climate can be extremely dark, too. Our sitting-room is to be in varnished wood. The room I have particularly in mind is a sort of bed and sitting room, pretty large, lit on three sides, and the colour in favour of its proprietor at present is a topazy yellow. But then with what colour to relieve it? For a little work-room of my own at the back I should rather like to see some patterns of unglossy—well, I'll be hanged if I can describe this red. It's not Turkish, and it's not Roman, and it's not Indian; but it seems to partake of the last two, and yet it can't be either of them, because it ought to be able to go with vermilion. Ah, what a tangled web we weave! Anyway, with what brains you have left choose me and send me some—many—patterns of the exact shade."

(1) Where could be found a more delightful cry for some rational way to describe color? He wants "a topazy yellow" and a red that is not Turkish nor Roman nor Indian, but that "seems to partake of the last two, and yet it can't be either of them." As a cap to the climax comes his demand for "patterns of the exact shade." Thus one of the clearest and most forceful writers of 10 English finds himself unable to describe the color he wants. And why? Simply because popular language does not clearly state a single one of the three qualities united in every color, and which must be known before one may even hope to convey his color conceptions to another.

(2) The incongruous and bizarre nature of our present color names must appear to any thoughtful person. Baby blue, peacock blue, Nile green, apple green, lemon yellow, straw yellow, rose pink, heliotrope, royal purple, Magenta, Solferino, plum, and automobile are popular terms, conveying different ideas to different persons and utterly failing to define colors. The terms used for a single hue, such as pea green, sea green, olive green, grass green, sage green, evergreen, invisible green, are not to be trusted in order-

ing a piece of cloth. They invite mistakes and disappointment. Not only are they inaccurate: they are inappropriate. Can we imagine musical tones called lark, canary, cockatoo, crow, cat, dog, or mouse, because they bear some distant resemblance to the cries of those animals? See paragraph 131.

Color needs a system.

(3) Music is equipped with a system by which it defines each sound in terms of its pitch, intensify, and duration, without dragging in loose allusions to the endlessly varying sounds of nature. So should color be supplied with an appropriate system, based on the hue, value, and chroma2 of our sensations, and not attempting to describe them by the indefinite and varying colors of natural objects. The system now to be considered portrays the three dimensions of color, and measures each by an appropriate scale. It does not rest upon the whim of an individual, but upon physical measurements made possible by special color 11 apparatus. The results may be tested by any one who comes to the problem with "a clear mind, agood eye, and a fair supply of patience."

Clear mental images make clear speech. Vague thoughts find vague utterance.

(4) The child gathers flowers, hoards colored beads, chases butterflies, and begs for the gaudiest painted toys. At first his strong color sensations are sufficiently described by the simple terms of red, yellow, green, blue, and purple. But he soon sees that some are light, while others are dark, and later comes to perceive that each hue has many grayer degrees. Now, if he wants to describe a particular red,—such as that of his faded cap,—he is not content to merely call it red, since he is aware of other red objects which are very unlike it. So he gropes for means to define this particular red; and, having no standard of comparison,—no scale by which to estimate,—he hesitatingly says it is a "sort of dull red."

(5) Thus early is he cramped by the poverty of color language. He has never been given an appropriate word for this color quality, and has to borrow one signifying the opposite of sharp, which belongs to edge tools rather than to colors.

Most color terms are borrowed from other senses.

(6) When his older sister refers to the "tone" of her green dress, or speaks of the "key of color" in a picture, he is naturally confused, because tone and key are terms associated in his mind with music. It may not be long before he will hear that "a color note has been pitched too high," or that a certain artist "paints in a minor key." All these terms lead to mixed and indefinite ideas, and leave him unequipped for the clear expression of color qualities.

(7) Musical art is not so handicapped. It has an established 12 scale with measured intervals and definite terms. Likewise, coloristic art must establish a scale, measure its intervals, and name its qualities in unmistakable fashion.

Color has three dimensions.

(8) It may sound strange to say that color has three dimensions, but it is easily proved by the fact that each of them can be measured. Thus in the case of the boy's faded cap its redness or HUE3 is determined by one instrument; the amount of light in the red, which is its VALUE,3 is found by another instrument; while still a third instrument determines the purity or CHROMA3 of the red.

The omission of any one of these three qualities leaves us in doubt as to the character of a color, just as truly as the character of this studio would remain undefined if the length were omitted and we described it as 22 feet wide by 14 feet high. The imagination would be free to ascribe any length it chose, from 25 to 100 feet. This length might be differently conceived by every individual who tried to supply the missing factor.

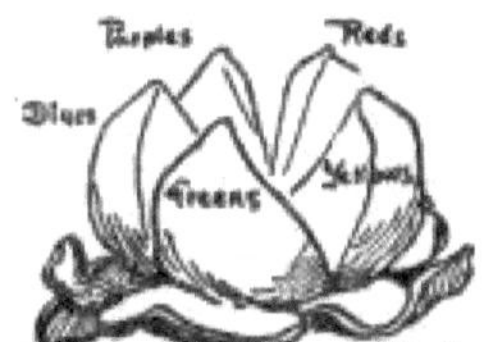

(9) To illustrate the tri-dimensional nature of colors. Suppose we peel an orange and divide it in five parts, leaving the sections slightly connected below (Fig.4). Then let us say that all the reds we have ever seen are gathered in one of the sections, all yellows in another, all greens in the third, blues in the

fourth, and purples in the fifth. Next we will assort these HUES in each section so that the lightest are near the top, and grade regularly to the darkest near the bottom. Awhite wafer connects all the sections at the top, and a black wafer may be added beneath. See PlateI.

(10) The fruit is then filled with assorted colors, graded from white to black, according to their VALUES, and disposed by their HUES in the five sections. Aslice near the top will uncover light values in all hues, and a slice near the bottom will find dark values in the same hues. Aslice across the middle discloses a circuit of hues all of MIDDLE VALUE; that is, midway between the extremes of white and black.

(11) Two color dimensions are thus shown in the orange, and it remains to exhibit the third, which is called CHROMA, or strength of color. To do this, we have only to take each section in turn, and, without disturbing the values already assorted, shove the grayest in toward the narrow edge, and grade outward to the purest on the surface. Each slice across the fruit still shows the circuit of hues in one uniform value; but the strong chromas are at the outside, while grayer and grayer chromas make a gradation inward to neutral gray at the centre, where all trace of color disappears. The thin edges of all sections unite in a scale of gray from black to white, no matter what hue each contains.

The curved outside of each section shows its particular hue graded from black to white; and, should the section be cut at right angles to the thin edge, it would show the third dimension,—chroma,—for the color is graded evenly from the surface to neutral gray. Apin stuck in at any point traces the third dimension.

A color sphere can be used to unite the three dimensions of hue, value, and chroma.

(12) 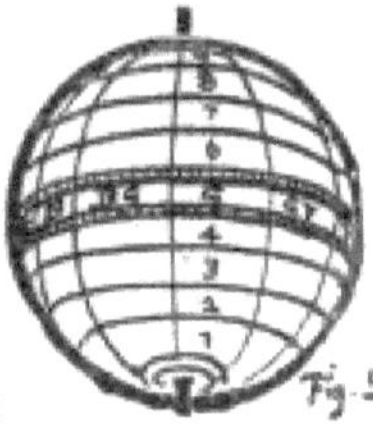 Having used the familiar structure of the orange as a help in classifying colors, let us substitute a geometric solid, like a sphere,4 and make use of geographical terms. The north pole is white. The south pole is black. 14 The equator is a circuit of middle reds, yellows, greens, blues, and purples. Parallels above the equator describe this circuit in lighter values, and parallels below trace it in darker values. The vertical axis joining black and white is a neutral scale of gray values, while perpendiculars to it (like a pin thrust into the orange) are scales of chroma. Thus our color notions may be brought into an orderly relation by the color sphere. Any color describes its light and strength by its location in the solid or on the surface, and is named by its place in the combined scales of hue, value, and chroma.

Two dimensions fail to describe a color.

(13) Much of the popular misunderstanding of color is caused by ignorance of these three dimensions or by an attempt to make two dimensions do the work of three.

(14) Flat diagrams showing hues and values, but omitting to define chromas, are as incomplete as would be a map of Switzerland with the mountains left out, or a harbor chart without indications of the depth of water. We find by aid of the measuring instruments that pigments are very unequal in this third dimension,—chroma,—producing mountains and valleys on the color sphere, so that, when the color system is worked out in pigments and charted, some colors must be traced well out beyond the spherical surface (paragraphs 125–127). Indeed, aCOLOR TREE5 is needed to display by the unequal levels and lengths of its branches the individuality of pigment colors. But, whatever solid or figure is used to illustrate color relations, it must combine the three scales of hue, value, and

chroma, and these definite scales furnish a name for every color based upon its intrinsic qualities, and free from terms purloined in other sensations, or caught from the fluctuating colors of natural objects.

How this system describes the spectrum.

(15) The solar spectrum and rainbow are the most stimulating color experiences with which we are acquainted. Can they be described by this solid system?

(16) The lightest part of the spectrum is a narrow field of greenish yellow, grading into darker red on one side and into darker green upon the other, followed by still darker blue and purple. Upon the sphere the values of these spectral colors trace a path high up on the yellow section, near white, and slanting downward across the red and green sections, which are traversed near the level of the equator, it goes on to cross the blue and purple well down toward black.

(17) This forms an inclined circuit, crossing the equator at opposite points, and suggests the ecliptic or the rings of Saturn (see outside cover). Apale rainbow would describe a slanting circuit nearer white, and a dimmer one would fall within the sphere, while an intensely brilliant spectrum projects far beyond the surface of the sphere, so greatly is the chroma of its hues in excess of the common pigments with which we work out our problems.

(18) At the outset it is well to recognize the place of the spectrum in this system, not only because it is the established basis of scientific study, but especially because the invariable order assumed by its hues is the only stable hint which Nature affords us in her infinite color play.

(19) All our color sensations are included in the color solid. None are left out by its scales of hue, value, and chroma. Indeed, the imagination is led to conceive and locate still purer colors than any we now possess. Such increased degrees of color sensation can be named, and clearly conveyed by symbols to another person as soon as the system is comprehended.

1. Vailima Letters, Oct. 8, 1902.

2. See color variables in Glossary.

3. For definitions of Hue, Value, and Chroma, see paragraphs 20–23.

4. See frontispiece.

5. For description of the Color Tree see paragraphs 33 and34.

16

Appendix to Chapter I.

Misnomers for Color.

The Century Dictionary helps an intelligent study of color by its clear definitions and cross-references to HUE, VALUE, and CHROMA,—leaving no excuse for those who would confuse these three qualities or treat a degree of any quality as the quality itself.

Obscure statements were frequent in text-books before these new definitions appeared. Thus the term "shade" should be applied only to darkened values, and not to hues or chromas. Yet one writer says, "This yellow shades into green," which is certainly a change of hue, and then speaks of "a brighter shade" in spite of his evident intention to suggest a stronger chroma, which is neither a shade nor brighter luminosity.

Children gain wrong notions of "tint and shade" from the so-called standard colors shown to them, which present "tints" of red and blue much darker than the "shades" of yellow. This is bewildering, and, like their elders, they soon drop into the loose habit of calling any degree of color-strength or color-light a "shade." *Value* is a better term to describe the light which color reflects to the eye, and all color values, light or dark, are measured by the *value-scale.*

"Tone" is used in a confusing way to mean different things. Thus in the same sentence we see it refers to a single touch of the brush,—which is not a tone, but a paint spot,—and then we 17 read that the "tone of the canvas is golden." This cannot mean that each paint spot is the color of gold, but is intended to suggest that the various objects depicted seem enveloped in a yellow atmosphere. Tone is, in fact, amusical term appropriate to sound, but out of place in color. It seems better to call the brush touch a *color-spot*: then the result of an harmonious relation between all the spots is *color-envelope*, or, as in Rood, "the chromatic composition."

"Intensity" is a misleading term, if chroma be intended, for it depends on the relative light of spectral hues. It is a degree rather than a quality, as appears in the expressions, intense heat, light, sound,—intensity of stimulus and reaction. Being a degree of many qualities, it should not be used to describe the quality itself. The word becomes especially unfit when used to describe two very different phases of a color,—as its intense illumination, where the chroma is greatly weakened, and the strongest chroma which is found in a much lower value. "Purity" is also to be avoided in speaking of pigments, for not one of our pigments represents a single pure ray of the spectrum.

Examples are constantly found of the mental blur caused by such unfortunate terms, and, since misunderstanding becomes impossible with measured degrees of hue, value, and chroma, it seems only a question of time when they will take the place of tint, tone, shade, purity and intensity.

Chapter II.
COLOR QUALITIES.

(20) The three color qualities are hue, value, and chroma.

HUE is the name of a color.

(21) Hue is the quality by which we distinguish one color from another, as a red from a yellow, agreen, ablue, or a purple. This names the hue, but does not tell whether it is light or dark, weak or strong,—leaving us in doubt as to its value and its chroma.

Science attributes this quality to difference in the LENGTH of ether waves impinging on the retina, which causes the sensation of color. The wave length M. 5269 gives a sensation of green, while M. 6867 gives a sensation of red.[6]

VALUE is the light of a color.

(22) Value is the quality by which we distinguish a light color from a dark one. Color values are loosely called tints and shades, but the terms are frequently misapplied. Atint should be a light value, and a shade should be darker; but the word "shade" has become a general term for any sort of color, so that a shade of yellow may prove to be lighter than a tint of blue. Aphotometric[7] scale of value places all colors in relation to the extremes of white and black, but cannot describe their hue or their chroma.

19

Science describes this quality as due to difference in the HEIGHT or amplitude of ether waves impinging on the retina. Small amplitudes of the wave lengths given in paragraph 21 produce the sensation of dark green and dark red: larger amplitudes give the sensation of lighter green and lighter red.

CHROMA is the strength of a color.

(23) Chroma is the quality by which we distinguish a strong color from a weak one. To say that a rug is strong in color gives no hint of its hues or values, only its chromas. Loss of chroma is loosely called

fading, but this word is frequently used to include changes of value and hue. Take two autumn leaves, identical in color, and expose one to the weather, while the other is waxed and pressed in a book. Soon the exposed leaf fades into a neutral gray, while the protected one preserves its strong chroma almost intact. If, in fading, the leaf does not change its hue or its value, there is only a loss of chroma, but the fading process is more likely to induce some change of the other two qualities. Fading, however, cannot define these changes.

Science describes chroma as the purity of one wave length separated from all others. Other wave lengths, INTERMINGLING, make its chroma less pure. Abeam of daylight can combine all wave lengths in such balance as to give the sensation of whiteness, because no single wave is in excess.8

(24) The color sphere (see Fig. 1) is a convenient model to illustrate these three qualities,—hue, value, and chroma,—and unite them by measured scales.

(25) The north pole of the color sphere is white, and the south pole black. Value or luminosity of colors ranges between these two extremes. This is the vertical scale, to be memorized as *V*, 20 the initial for both value and vertical. Vertical movement through color may thus be thought of as a change of value, but not as a change of hue or of chroma. Hues of color are spread around the equator of the sphere. This is a horizontal scale, memorized as *H*, the initial for both hue and horizontal. Horizontal movement around the color solid is thus thought of as a change of hue, but not of value or of chroma. Aline inward from the strong surface hues to the neutral gray axis, traces the graying of each color, which is loss of chroma, and conversely a line beginning with neutral gray at the vertical axis, and becoming more and more colored until it passes outside the sphere, is a scale of chroma, which is memorized as C, the initial both for chroma and centre. Thus the sphere lends its three dimensions to color description, and a color

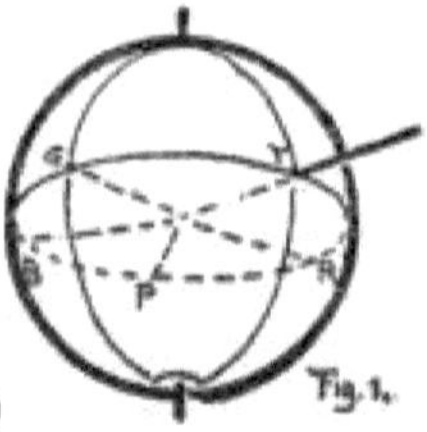

applied anywhere within, without, or on its surface is located and named by its degree of hue, of value, and of chroma.

HUES first appeal to the child, VALUES next, and CHROMAS last.

(26) Color education begins with ability to recognize and name certain hues, such as red, yellow, green, blue, and purple (see paragraphs 182 and 183). Nature presents these hues in union with such varieties of value and chroma that, unless there be some standard of comparison, it is impossible for one person to describe them intelligently to another.

(27) The solar spectrum forms a basis for scientific color analysis, taught in technical schools; but it is quite beyond the comprehension of a child. He needs something more tangible and constantly in view to train his color notions. He needs to handle colors, place them side by side for comparison, imitate them with 21 crayons, paints, and colored stuffs, so as to test the growth of perception, and learn by simple yet accurate terms to describe each by its hue, its value, and its chroma.

(28) Pigments, rather than the solar spectrum, are the practical agents of color work. Certain of them, selected and measured by this system (see Chapter V.), will be known as MIDDLE COLORS, because they stand midway in the scales of value and chroma. These middle colors are preserved in imperishable enamels,9 so that the child may handle and fix them in his memory, and thus gain a permanent basis for comparing all degrees of color. He learns to grade each middle color to its extremes of value and chroma.

(29) Experiments with crayons and paints, and efforts to match middle colors, train his color sense to finer perceptions. Having learned to name colors, he compares them with the enamels of middle value, and can describe how light or dark they are. Later he perceives their differences of strength, and, comparing them with the enamels of middle chroma, can describe how weak or strong they are. Thus the full significance of these middle colors as a practical basis for all color estimates becomes apparent; and, when at a more advanced stage he studies the best examples of decorative

color, he will again encounter them in the most beautiful products of Oriental art.

22

Is it possible to define the endless varieties of color?

(30) At first glance it would seem almost hopeless to attempt the naming of every kind and degree of color. But, if all these varieties possess the same three qualities, only in different degrees, and if each quality can be measured by a scale, then there is a clue to this labyrinth.

A COLOR SPHERE and COLOR TREE to unite hue, value, and chroma.

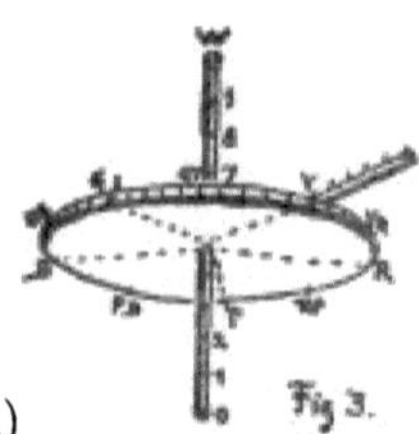

(31) This clue is found in the union of these three qualities by measured scales in a *color sphere and color tree.*10 The equator of the sphere11 may be divided into ten parts, and serve as the scale of hue, markedR, YR,Y, GY,G, BG,B, PB, P, and RP. Its vertical axis may be divided into ten parts to serve as the scale of value, numbered from black (0) to white (10). Any perpendicular to the neutral axis is a scale of chroma. On the plane of the equator this scale is numbered 1, 2, 3, 4, 5, from the centre to the surface.

(32) This chroma scale may be raised or lowered to any level of value, always remaining perpendicular to the axis, and serving to measure the chroma of every hue at every level of value. The fact that some colors exceed others to such an extent as to carry them out beyond the sphere is proved by measuring instruments, 23 but the fact is a new one to many persons. (Figs. 2 and3.)

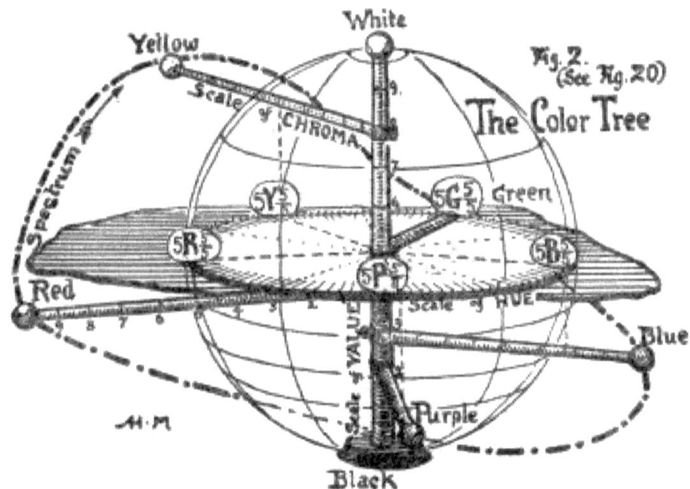

(33) For this reason the COLOR TREE is a completer model than the sphere, although the simplicity of the latter makes it best for a child's comprehension.

(34) The color tree is made by taking the vertical axis of the sphere, which carries a scale of value, for the trunk. The branches are at right angles to the trunk; and, as in the sphere, they carry the scale of chroma. Colored balls on the branches tell their Hue. In order to show the MAXIMA of color, each branch is attached to the trunk (or neutral axis) at a level demanded by its value,—the yellow nearest white at the top, then the green, red, blue, and purple branches, approaching black in the order of their lower values. It will be remembered that the chroma of the sphere ceased with 5 at the equator. The color tree prolongs 24 this through 6, 7, 8, and9. The branch ends carry colored balls, representing the most powerful red, yellow, green, blue, and purple pigments which we now possess, and could be lengthened, should stronger chromas be discovered.12

(35) Such models set up a permanent image of color relations. Every point is self-described by its place in the united scales of hue, value, and chroma. These scales fix each new perception of color in the child's mind by its situation in the color solid. The importance of such a definite image can hardly be overestimated, for without it

one color sensation tends to efface another. When the child looks at a color, and has no basis of comparison, it soon leaves a vague memory that cannot be described. These models, on the contrary, lead to an intelligent estimate of each color in terms of its hue, its value, and its chroma; while the permanent enamels correct any personal bias by a definite standard.

(36) Thus defined, a color falls into logical relation with all other colors in the system, and is easily memorized, so that its image may be recalled at any distance of time or place by the notation.

(37) These solid models help to memorize and assemble colors and the memory is further strengthened by a simple NOTATION, which records each color so that it cannot be mistaken for any other. By these written scales a child gains an instinctive estimate of relations, so that, when he is delighted with a new color combination, its proportions are noted and understood.

(38) Musical art has long enjoyed the advantages of a definite scale and notation. Should not the art of coloring gain by similar definition? The musical scale is not left to personal 25 whim, nor does it change from day to day; and something as clear and stable would be an advantage in training the color sense.

(39) Perception of color is crude at first. The child sees only the most obvious distinctions, and prefers the strongest stimulation. But perception soon becomes refined by exercise, and, when a child tries to imitate the subtle colors of nature with paints, he begins to realize that the strongest colors are not the most beautiful,—rather the tempered ones, which may be compared to the moderate sounds in music. To describe these tempered colors, he must estimate their hue, value, and chroma, and be able to describe in what degree his copy departs from the natural color. And, with this gain in perception and imitation of natural color, he finds a strong desire to invent combinations to please his fancy. Thus the study divides into three related attitudes, which may be called recognition, imitation, and invention. Recognition of color is fundamental, but it would be tedious to spend a year or two in formal and dry exercises to train recognition of color alone; for each step in recognition of color is best tested by exercise in its imitation and arrangement. When perception becomes keener, emphasis can be placed on imitation of the

colors found in art and in nature, resting finally on the selection and grouping of colors for design.13

Every color can be recognized, named, matched, imitated, and written by its HUE, VALUE, and CHROMA.

(40) The notation used in this system places Hue (expressed by an initial) at the left; Value (expressed by a number) at the right and above a line; and Chroma (also expressed by 26 a number) at the right, below the line. Thus $R^5/_9$ means

HUE(red), $\frac{\text{VALUE (5)}}{\text{CHROMA(9)}}$, and will be found to represent the qualities of the pigment vermilion.14

Hue, value, and chroma unite in every color sensation, but the child cannot grasp them all at once. *Hue-difference appeals to him first,* and he gains a permanent idea of five principal hues from the enamels of MIDDLE COLORS, learning to name, match, imitate, and finally write them by their initials: R (red), Y (yellow), G (green), B (blue), and P (purple). Intermediates formed by uniting successive pairs are also written by the joined initials, YR (yellow-red), GY (green-yellow), BG (blue-green), PB (purple-blue), and RP (red-purple).

(41) Ten differences of hue are as many as a child can render at the outset, yet in matching and imitating them he becomes aware of their light and dark quality, and learns to separate it from hue as *value-difference.* Middle colors, as implied by that name, stand midway between white and black,—that is, on the equator of the sphere,—so that a middle red will be written $R^5/$, suggesting the steps 6, 7, 8, and 9 which are above the equator, while steps 4, 3, 2, and 1 are below. It is well to show only three values of a color at first; for instance, the middle value contrasted with a light and a dark one. These are written $R^3/$, $R^5/$, $R^7/$. Soon he perceives and can imitate finer differences, and the red scale may be written entire, as $R^1/$, $R^2/$, $R^3/$, $R^4/$, $R^5/$, $R^6/$, $R^7/$, $R^8/$, $R^9/$, with black as 0 and white as10.

(42)*Chroma-difference is the third* and most subtle color quality. The child is already unconsciously familiar with the middle chroma of red, having had the enamels of MIDDLE COLOR always 27 in view, and the red enamel is to be contrasted with the strongest and weakest red chromas obtainable. These he writes $R/_1$, $R/5$, $R/_9$, seeing that this describes the chromas of red, but leaves out its values. $R^5/_1$, $R^5/_5$, $R^5/_9$, is the complete statement, showing that, while both hue and value are unchanged, the chroma passes from grayish red to middle red (enamel first learned) and out to the strongest red in the chroma scale obtained by vermilion.

(43) It may be long before he can imitate the intervening steps of chroma, many children finding it difficult to express more than five steps of the chroma scale, although easily making ten steps of value and from twenty to thirty-five steps of hue. This interesting feature is of psychologic value, and has been followed in the color tree and color sphere.

Does such a scientific scheme leave any outlet for feeling and personal expression of beauty?

(44) Lest this exact attitude in color study should seem inartistic, compared with the free and almost chaotic methods in use, let it be said that the stage thus far outlined is frankly disciplinary. It is somewhat dry and unattractive, just as the early musical training is fatiguing without inventive exercises. The child should be encouraged at each step to exercise his fancy.

(45) Instead of cramping his outlook upon nature, it widens his grasp of color, and stores the memory with finer differences, supplying more material by which to express his sense of coloristic beauty.

(46) Color harmony, as now treated, is a purely personal affair, difficult to refer to any clear principles or definite laws. The very terms by which it seeks expression are borrowed from music, and suggest vague analogies that fail when put to the test. Color 28 needs a new set of expressive terms, appropriate to its qualities, before we can make an analysis as to the harmony or discord of our color sensations.

(47) This need is supplied in the present system by measured CHARTS, and a NOTATION. Their very construction preserves the *balance of colors*, as will be shown in the next chapter, while the chapter on harmony (Chapter VII.) shows how harmonious pairs

and triads of color may be found by MASKS with measured intervals. In fact, practice in the use of the charts supplies the imagination with scales and sequences of color quite as definite and quite as easily written as those sound intervals by which the musician conveys to others his sense of harmony. And, although in neither art can training alone make the artist, yet a technical grasp of these formal scales gives acquaintance with the full range of the instrument, and is indispensable to artistic expression. From these color scales each individual is free to choose combinations in accord with his feeling for color harmony.

Let us make an outline of the course of color study traced in the preceding pages.15

PERCEPTION of color.

(48)*Hue-difference.*

Middle hues (5 principals).

Middle hues (5 intermediates).

Middle hues (10 placed in sequence as SCALE of HUE).

Value-difference.

Light, middle, and dark values (without change of hue).

Light, middle, and dark values (traced with 5 principal hues).

10 values traced with each hue. SCALE of VALUE. *The Color Sphere.*

29

Chroma-difference.

Strong, middle, and weak chroma (without change of hue).

Strong, middle and weak chroma (traced with three values without change of hue).

Strong, middle, and weak chroma (traced with three values and ten hues).

Maxima of color and their gradation to white, black, and gray. *The Color Tree.*

EXPRESSION of color.

(49)*Matching and imitation* of hues (using stuffs, crayons, and paints).

Matching and imitation of values and hues (using stuffs, crayons, and paints).

Matching and imitation of chromas, values, and hues (using stuffs, crayons, and paints).

Notation of color.

$$\text{Hue}\,\frac{\text{Value}}{\text{Chroma}},\; H\frac{V}{C},$$

Initial for hue, numeral above for value, numeral below for chroma.

Sequences of color.

Two scales united, as hue and value, or chroma and value.

Three scales united,—each step a change of hue, value, and chroma.

Balance of color.

Opposites of equal value and chroma ($R^{5}/_{5}$ and $BG^{5}/_{5}$).

Opposites of equal value and unequal chroma ($R^{5}/_{9}$ and $BG^{5}/_{3}$).

Opposites unequal both in value and chroma ($R^{7}/_{3}$ and $BG^{3}/_{7}$).

AREA as an element of balance.

HARMONY of color.

(50)*Selection of colors* that give pleasure.

Study of butterfly wings and flowers, recorded by the NOTATION.

Study of painted ornament, rugs, and mosaics, recorded by the NOTATION.

Personal choice of color PAIRS, balanced by H, V, C, and area.

Personal choice of color TRIADS, balanced by H, V, C, and area.

Grouping of colors to suit some practical use: wall papers, rugs, book covers, etc.

Their analysis by the written notation.

Search for principles of harmony, expressed in measured terms.

A definite plan of color study, with freedom as to details of presentation.16

(51) Having memorized these broad divisions of the study, aclever teacher will introduce many a detail, to meet the mood of the class, or correlate this subject with other studies, without for a moment losing the thread of thought or befogging the presentation. But to range at random in the immense field of color sensations, without plan or definite aim in view, only courts fatigue of the retina and a chaotic state of mind.

(52) The same broad principles which govern the presentation of other ideas apply with equal force in this study. Alittle, well apprehended, is better than a mass of undigested facts. If the child is led to discover, or at least to think he is discovering, new things about color, the mind will be kept alert and seek out novel illustrations at every step. Now and then a pupil will be found 31 who leads both teacher and class by *intuitive* appreciation of color, and it is a subtle question how far such a nature can be helped or hurt by formal exercises. But such an exception is rare, and goes to prove that systematic discipline of the color sense is necessary for most children.

(53) Outdoor nature and indoor surroundings offer endless color illustrations. Birds, flowers, minerals, and the objects in daily use take on a new interest when their varied colors are brought into a conscious relation, and clearly named. Atri-dimensional perception, like this sense of color, requires skilful training, and each lesson must be simplified to the last point practicable. It must not be too long, and should lead to some definite result which a child can grasp and express with tolerable accuracy, while its difficulties should be approached by easy stages, so as to avoid failure or discouragement. The success of the present effort is the best incentive to further achievement.

6. See Glossary for definitions of Micron, Photometer, Retina, and Red, also for Hue, Tint, Shade, Value, Color Variables, Luminosity, and Chroma.

7. See Photometer in paragraph 65.

8. See definition of White in Glossary.

9. When recognized for the first time, amiddle green, blue, or purple, is accepted by most persons as well within their color habit, but middle red and middle yellow cause somewhat of a shock. "That isn't red," they say, "it's terra cotta." "Yellow?" "Oh, no, that's—well, it's a very peculiar shade."

Yet these are as surely the middle degrees of red and yellow as are the more familiar degrees of green, blue, and purple. This becomes evident as soon as one accepts physical tests of color in place of personal whim. It also opens the mind to a generally ignored fact, that middle reds and yellows, instead of the screaming red and yellow first given a child, are constantly found in examples of rich and beautiful color, such as Persian rugs, Japanese prints, and the masterpieces of painting.

10. See Color Tree in paragraph14.

11. Unaware that the spherical arrangement had been used years before, Idevised a double tetrahedron to classify colors, while a student of painting in 1879. It now appears that the sphere was common property with psychologists, having been described by Runge in 1810. Earlier still, Lambert had suggested a pyramidal form. Both are based on the erroneous assumption that red, yellow, and blue are primary sensations, and also fail to place these hues in a just scale of luminosity. My twirling color solid and its completer development in the present model have always made prominent the artistic feeling for color value. It differs in this and in other ways from previous systems, and is fortunate in possessing new apparatus to measure the degree of hue, value, and chroma.

12. See Plate I.

13. See Course of Study, Part II.

14. See Chapter VI.

15.*See* Part II., A Color System and Course of Study.

16. See Color Study assigned to each grade, in PartII.

32

Appendix to Chapter II.
PLATE I.
THE COLOR SPHERE, with Measured Scales of HUE, VALUE, and CHROMA.

The teacher of elementary grades introduces these scales of tempered color as fast as the child's interest is awakened to their need by the exercises shown in Plates II. and III. Thus the Hue scale is learned before the end of the second year, the Value scale during the next two years, and the Chroma scale in the fifth year. By the time a child is ten years old these definite color scales have become part of his mental furnishing, so that he can name, write, and memorize any color group.

1. *The Color Sphere in Skeleton.* This diagram shows the middle colors on the equator, with strong red, yellow, green, blue, and purple, each at its proper level in the value scale, and projecting in accordance with its scale of chroma. See the complete description of these scales in ChapterII.

2. *The Color Score.* Fifteen typical steps taken from the color sphere are here spread out in a flat field. The FIVE MIDDLE COLORS form the centre level, with the same hues in a lighter value above and in a darker value below. Chapter VI. describes the making of this Score, and its use in analyzing colors and preserving a written record of their groups.

3. *The Value Scale and Chroma Scale.* Each of the five color maxima is thus shown at its proper level in the scale of light, and graded by uniform steps from its strongest chroma inward to neutrality at the axis of the sphere. Pigment inequalities here become very apparent.

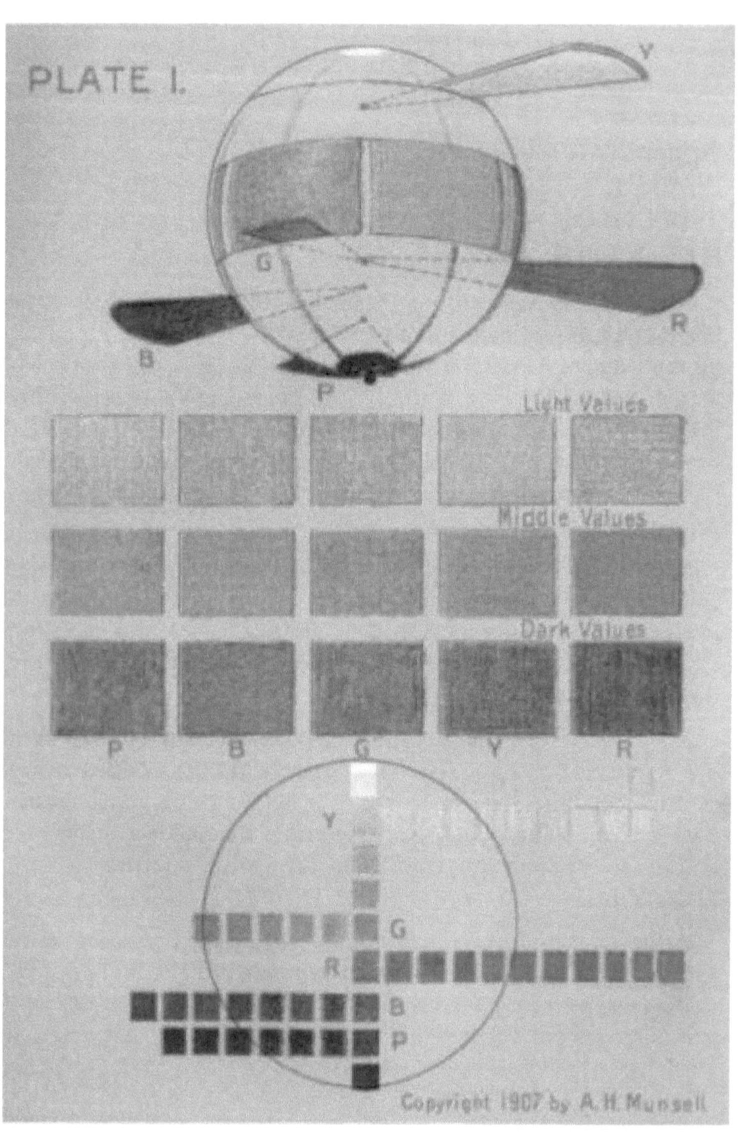
PLATE I.
Y
G
B
R
P
Light Values
Middle Values
Dark Values
P
B
G
Y
R
Y
G
R
B
P
Copyright 1907 by A. H. Munsell

33

FOR PLATES II. & III.,
SEE APPENDIX TO CHAPTER IV.,
CHILDREN'S COLOR STUDIES.

34

Chapter III.
COLOR MIXTURE AND BALANCE.

All colors grasped in the hand.

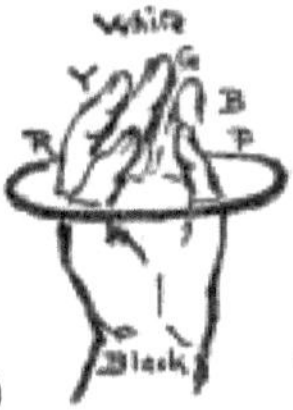

(54) Let us recall the names and order of colors given in the last chapter, with their assemblage in a sphere by the three qualities of HUE, VALUE, and CHROMA. It will aid the memory to call the thumb of the left hand RED, the forefinger YELLOW, the middle finger GREEN, the ring finger BLUE, and the little finger PURPLE (Fig.6). When the finger tips are in a circle, they represent a circuit of hues, which has neither beginning nor end, for we can start with any finger and trace a sequence forward or backward. Now close the tips together for white, and imagine that the five strong hues have slipped down to the knuckles, where they stand for the equator of the color Sphere. Still lower down at the wrist is black.

(55) The hand thus becomes a color holder, with white at the finger tips, black at the wrist, strong colors around the outside, and weaker colors within the hollow. Each finger is a scale of its own color, with white above and black below, while the graying of all the hues is traced by imaginary lines which meet in the middle of the hand. Thus a child's hand may be his substitute for the color sphere, and also make him realize that it is filled with grayer degrees of the outside colors, all of which melt into gray in the centre.

Neighborly and opposite hues; and their mixture.

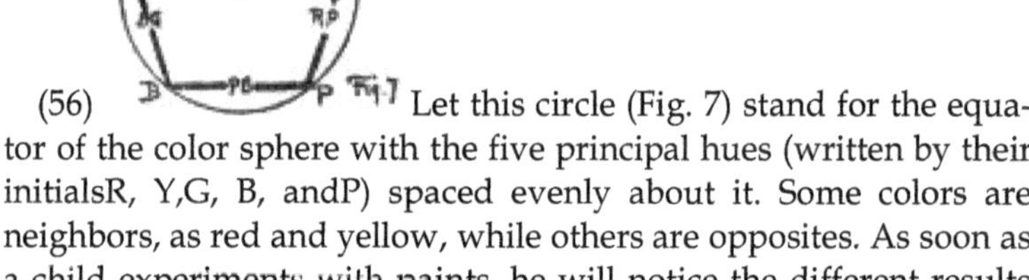

(56) Let this circle (Fig. 7) stand for the equator of the color sphere with the five principal hues (written by their initialsR, Y,G, B, andP) spaced evenly about it. Some colors are neighbors, as red and yellow, while others are opposites. As soon as a child experiments with paints, he will notice the different results obtained by mixing them.

First, the neighbors, that is, any pair which lie next one another, as red and yellow, will unite to make a hue which retains a suggestion of both. It is *intermediate* between red and yellow, and we call it YELLOW-RED.[17]

(57) Green and yellow unite to form GREEN-YELLOW, blue and green make BLUE-GREEN, and so on with each succeeding pair. These intermediates are to be written by their initials, and inserted in their proper place between the principal hues. It is as if an orange (paragraph9) were split into ten sectors instead of five, with red, yellow, green, blue, and purple as alternate sectors, while half of each adjoining color pair were united to form the sector between them. The original order of five hues is in no wise disturbed, but linked together by five intermediate steps.

(58) Here is a table of the intermediates made by mixing each pair:—

Red and yellow unite to form yellow-red (YR), popularly called orange.[17]

Yellow and green unite to form green-yellow (GY), popularly called grass green.

Green and blue unite to form blue-green (BG), popularly called peacock blue.

Blue and purple unite to form purple-blue (PB), popularly called violet.

Purple and red unite to form red-purple (RP), popularly called plum.

36

Using the left hand again to hold colors, the principal hues remain unchanged on the knuckles, but in the hollows between them are placed intermediate hues, so that the circle now reads: red, yellow-red, yellow, green-yellow, green, blue-green, blue, purple-blue, purple, and red-purple, back to the red with which we started. This circuit is easily *memorized*, so that the child may begin with any color point, and repeat the series clock wise (that is, from left to right) or in reverse order.

(59) Each principal hue has thus made two close neighbors by mixing with the nearest principal hue on either hand. The neighbors of red are a yellow-red on one side and a purple-red on the other. The neighbors of green are a green-yellow on one hand and a blue-green on the other. It is evident that a still closer neighbor could be made by again mixing each consecutive pair in this circle of ten hues; and, if the process were continued long enough, the color steps would become so fine that the eye could see only a circuit of hues melting imperceptibly one into another.

(60) But it is better for the child to gain a fixed idea of red, yellow, green, blue, and purple, with their intermediates, before attempting to mix pigments, and these ten steps are sufficient for primary education.

(61) Next comes the question of opposites in this circle. Aline drawn from red, through the centre, finds its opposite, blue-green.18 If these colors are mixed, they unite to form gray. Indeed, the centre of the circle stands for a middle gray, not only because it is the centre of the neutral axis between black and white, but also because any pair of opposites will unite to form gray.

37

(62) This is a table of five mixtures which make neutral gray:

	Red &	Blue-green	
Opposites	Yellow	Purple-blue	Each pair of which unites in neutral gray.
	Green	Red-purple	

Blue	Yellow-red
Purple	Green-yellow

(63) But if, instead of mixing these opposite hues, we place them side by side, the eye is so stimulated by their difference that each seems to gain in strength; *i.e.*, each *enhances* the other when separate, but *destroys* the other when mixed. This is a very interesting point to be more fully illustrated by the help of a color wheel in Chapter V., paragraph 106. What we need to remember is that the mixture of neighborly hues makes them less stimulating to the eye, because they resemble each other, while a mixture of opposite hues extinguishes both in a neutral gray.

Hues once removed, and their mixture.

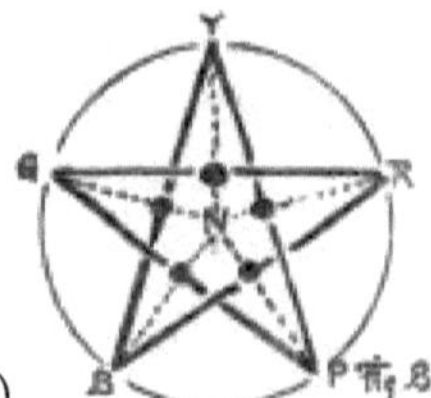

(64) There remains the question, What will happen if we mix, not two neighbors, nor two opposites, but *a pair of hues once removed in the circle*, such as red and green? Aline joining this pair does not pass through the neutral centre, but to one side nearer yellow, which shows that this mixture falls between neutral gray and yellow, partaking somewhat of each. In the same way a line joining yellow and blue shows that their mixture contains both green and gray. Indeed, aline joining any two colors in the circuit may be said to describe their union. Aradius crossing this line passes to some hue on the circumference, and describes by its intersection with the first line 38 the chroma of the color made by a mixture of the two original colors.

Red&	Greenmake	Yellow-gray
Yellow	Blue	Green-gray
Green	Purple	Blue-gray
Blue	Red	Purple-gray
Purple	Yellow	Red-gray

Each pair unites in a *colored* gray, which is an intermediate hue of weak chroma.

Mixture of white and black: ascale of grays.

(65) So far we have thought only of the plane of the equator, with its circle of middle hues in ten steps, and studied their mixture by drawing lines to join them. Now let us start at the neutral centre, and think upward to white and downward to black (Fig.9.)

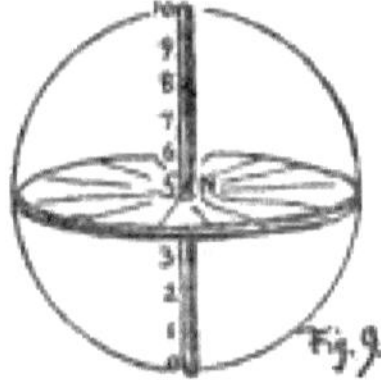

This vertical line is the *neutral axis* joining the poles of white and black, which represent the opposites of light and darkness. Middle gray is half-way between. If black is called 0, and white is 10, then the middle point is 5, with 6, 7, 8, and 9 above, while 4, 3, 2, and 1 are below, thus making a vertical scale of grays from black to white (Chapter II., paragraph25).

If left to personal preference, an estimate of middle value will vary with each individual who attempts to make it. This appears in the neutral scales already published for schools, and students who depend upon them, discover a variation of over 10 per cent. in the selection of middle gray. Since this VALUE SCALE underlies all color work, it needs accurate adjustment by scientific means, as in scales of sound, of length, of weight, or of temperature.

A PHOTOMETER (*photo*, light, and *meter*, ameasure)19 is shown 39 on the next page. It measures the relative amount of light which the eye receives from any source, and so enables us to make a scale with any number of regular steps. The principle on which it acts is very simple.

A rectangular box, divided by a central partition into halves, has symmetrical openings in the front walls, which permit the light to reach two white fields placed upon the back walls. If one looks in through the observation tube, both halves are seen to be exactly alike, and the white fields equally illuminated. Avalve is then fitted to one of the front openings, so that the light in that half of the photometer may be gradually diminished. Its white field is thus darkened by measured degrees, and becomes black when all light is excluded by the closed valve. While this darkening process goes on in one-half of the instrument, the white field in the other half does not change, and, looking into the eyepiece, the observer sees each step contrasted with the original white. One-half is thus said to be *variable* because of its valve, and the other side is said to be *fixed.* Adial connected with the valve has a hand moving over it to show how much light is admitted to the field in the variable half.

Let us now test one of these personal decisions about middle value. Asample replaces the white field in the fixed half, and by means of the valve, the white field in the variable half is alternately darkened and lightened, until it matches the sample and the eye sees no difference in the two. The dial then discloses the fact that this supposedly MIDDLE VALUE reflects only 42 per cent. of the light; that is to say, it is nearly a whole step too low in a decimal scale. Other samples err nearly as far on the light side of middle value, and further tests prove not only the varying color sensitiveness of individuals, but detect a difference between the left and right eye of the same person.

PHOTOMETER.

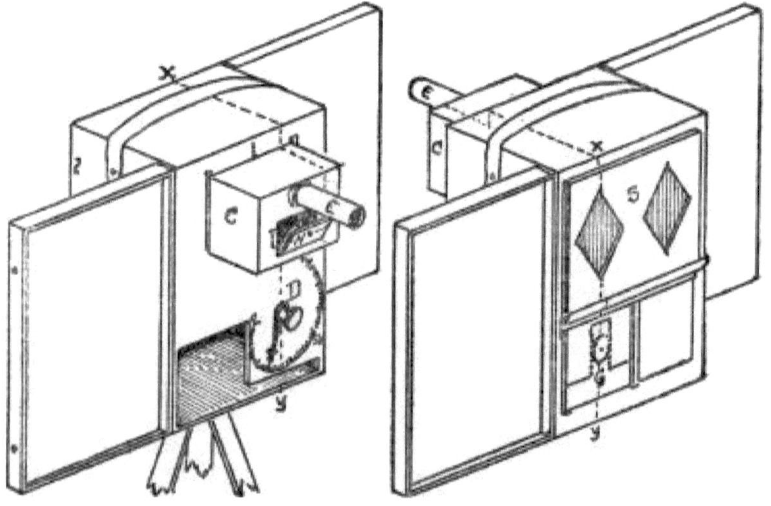

Back View. Front View.

The vagaries of color estimate thus disclosed, lead some to seek shelter in "feeling and inspiration"; but feeling and inspiration are temperamental, and have nothing to do with the simple facts of vision. Ameasured and unchanging scale is as necessary and valuable in the training of the eye as the musical scale in the discipline of the ear.

It will soon be necessary to talk of the values in each color. We may distinguish the values on the neutral axis from color values by writing them N^1, N^2, N^3, N^4, N^5, N^6, N^7, N^8, N^9, N^{10}. Such a scale makes it easy to foresee the result of mixing light values with dark ones. Any two gray values unite to form a gray midway between them. Thus N^4 and N^6 being equally above and below the centre, unite to form N^5, as will also $N^7$41 and N^3, N^8 and N^2, or N^9 and N^1. But N^9 and N^3 will unite to form N^6, which is midway between 6 and9.

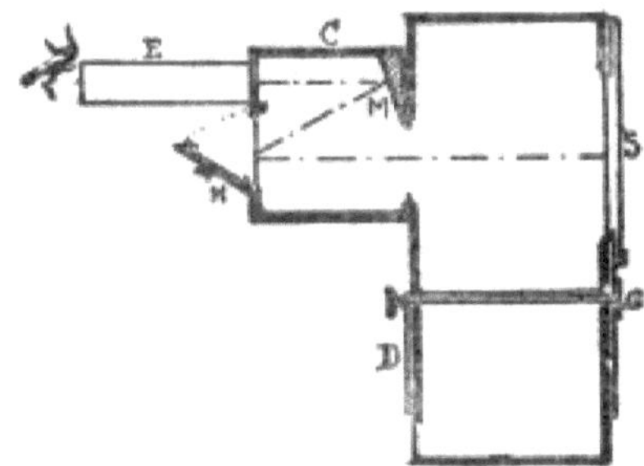

Vertical Section through light openings.

PARTS.

C, Cabinet, with sample-holder (H) and mirror (M), which may be removed and stored to left of dial (D) when instrument is closed for transportation.

D, Dial: records color values in terms of standard white (100), the opposite end of the scale being absolute blackness(0).

E, Eye-piece: to shield eye and sample from extraneous light while color determinations are being made. Fatigue of retina should be avoided.

G, GEAR: actuates cat's-eye shutter, which controls amount of light admitted to right half of instrument. Its shaft carries index-hand over dial.

H, FIELD-HOLDER: retains sample and standard white in same plane, and isolates them. Is hinged upon lower edge, and secured by pivot clamp.

M, MIRROR: permits observation of the isolated halves of the holder, bearing standard white and the color to be measured. Should be clean and free from dust on both sides of central partition.

S, DIFFUSING SCREEN, placed over front apertures, to evenly distribute the light.

(66) When this numbered scale of values is familiar, it serves not only to describe light and dark grays, but the value of colors which are at the same level in the scale. Thus R^7 (popularly called a tint of red) is neither lighter nor darker than the gray of N^7. Anumeral written above to the right always indicates *value,* whether of a gray or a color, so that R^1, R^2, R^3, R^4, R^5, R^6, R^7, R^8, R^9, describes a regular scale of red values from black to white, while G^1, G^2, G^3, etc., is a scale of green values.

42

(67) This matter of a notation for colors will be more fully worked out in Chapter VI., but the letters and numerals already described greatly simplify what we are about to consider in the mixture and balance of colors.

Mixture of light hues with dark hues.

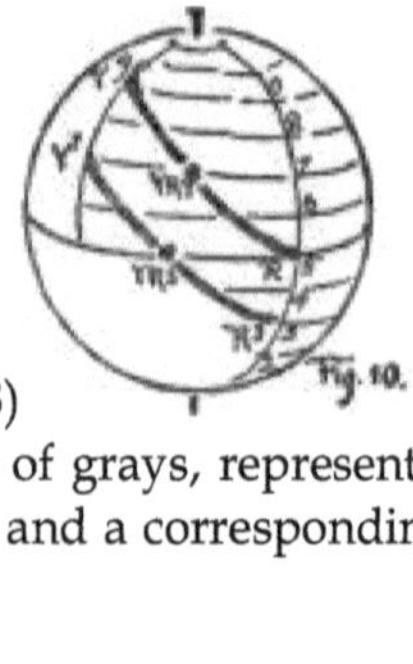

(68) Now that we are supplied with a decimal scale of grays, represented by divisions of the neutral axis (N^1, N^2, etc.), and a corresponding decimal scale of value for each of the ten

hues ranged about the equator (R^1, R^2,—YR^1, YR^2,—Y^1, Y^2,—GY^1, GY^2,—and so on), traced by ten equidistant meridians from black to white, it is not difficult to foresee what the mixture of any two colors will produce, whether they are of the same level of value, as in the colors of the equator already considered, or whether they are of different levels.

(69) For instance, let us mix a light yellow (Y^7) with a dark red (R^3). They are neighbors in hue, but well removed in value. Aline joining them centres at YR^5. This describes the result of their mixture,—a value intermediate between 7 and 3, with a hue intermediate between R andY. It is a yellow-red of middle value, popularly called "dark orange." But, while this term "dark orange" rarely means the same color to three different people, these measured scales give to YR^5 an unmistakable meaning, just as the musical scale gives an unmistakable significance to the notes of its score.

(70) Evidently, this way of writing colors by their degrees of value and hue gives clearness to what would otherwise be hard to express by the color terms in common use.

(71) If Y^9 and R^5 be chosen for mixture, we know at once that 43 they unite in YR^7, which is two steps of the value scale above the middle; while Y^6 and R^2 make YR^4, which is one step below the middle. Charts prepared with this system show each of these colors and their mixture with exactness.

(72) The foregoing mixtures of dark reds and light yellows are typical of the union of light and dark values of any neighboring hues, such as yellow and green, green and blue, blue and purple, or purple and red. Next let us think of the result of mixing different values in opposite hues; as, for instance, YR^7 and B^3 (Fig. 11). To this combination the color sphere gives a ready answer; for the middle of a straight line through the sphere, and joining them, coincides with the neutral centre, showing that they *balance in neutral gray*. This is also true of any opposite pair of surface hues where the values are equally removed from the equator.

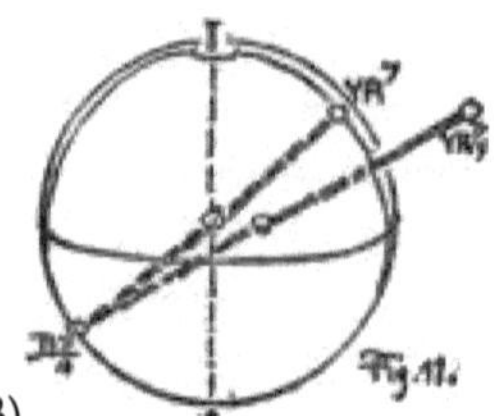

(73) Suppose we substitute familiar flowers for the notation, then YR^7 becomes the buttercup, and B^3 is the wild violet. But, in comparing the two, the eye is more stimulated by the buttercup than by the violet, not alone because it is lighter, but because it is stronger in chroma; that is, farther away from the neutral axis of the sphere, and in fact out beyond its surface, as shown in Fig.11.

The head of a pin stuck in toward the axis on the 7th level of YR may represent the 9th step in the scale of chroma, such as the buttercup, while the "modest" violet with a chroma of only 4, is shown by its position to be nearer the neutral axis than the brilliant buttercup by five steps of chroma. This is the third dimension of color, and must be included in our notation. 44 So we write the buttercup $YR^7/_9$ and the violet $B^3/_4$,—chroma always being written below to the right of hue, and value always above.

(This is the invariable order: HUE $\frac{\text{VALUE}}{\text{CHROMA}}$.)

(74) A line joining the head of the pin mentioned above with $B^3/_4$ does not pass through the centre of the sphere, and its middle point is nearer the buttercup than the neutral axis, showing that the hues of the buttercup and violet *do not balance in gray*.

The neutral centre is a balancing point for colors.

(75) This raises the question, What is balance of color? Artists criticise the color schemes of paintings as being "too light or too dark" (unbalanced in value), "too weak or too strong" (unbalanced in chroma), and "too hot or too cold" (unbalanced in hue), showing that this is a fundamental idea underlying all color arrangements.

(76) Let us assume that the centre of the sphere is the natural balancing point for all colors (which will be best shown by Maxwell

discs in Chapter V., paragraphs 106–112), then color points equally removed from the centre must balance one another. Thus white balances black. Lighter red balances darker blue-green. Middle red balances middle blue-green. In short, every straight line through this centre indicates opposite qualities that balance one another. The color points so found are said to be "*complementary,*" for each supplies what is needed to complement or balance the other in hue, value, and chroma.

(77) The true complement of the buttercup, then, is not the violet, which is too weak in chroma to balance its strong opposite. We have no blue flower that can equal the chroma of the buttercup. Some other means must be found to produce a balance. One way is to use more of the weaker color. Thus we can make 45 a bunch of buttercups and violets, using twice as many of the latter, so that the eye sees an *area* of blue twice as great as the *area* of yellow-red. Area as a compensation for inequalities of hue, value, and chroma will be further described under the harmony of color in Chapter VII.

(78) But, before leaving this illustration of the buttercup and violet, it is well to consider another color path connecting them which does not pass through the sphere, *but around it* (Fig. 12). Such a path swinging around from yellow-red to blue slants downward in value, and passes through yellow, green-yellow, green, and blue-green, tracing a *sequence of hue,* of which each step is less chromatic than its predecessor.

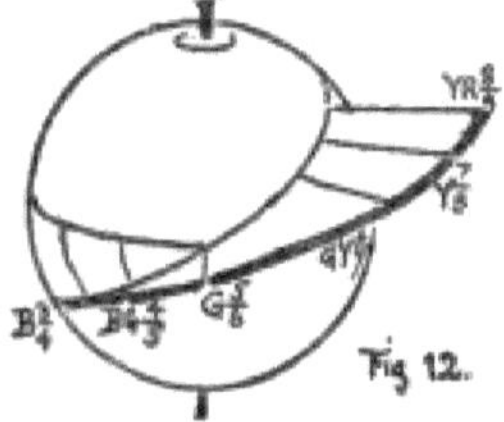

This diminishing sequence is easily written thus,—$YR^{8}/_{9}$, $Y^{7}/_{8}$, $GY^{6}/_{7}$, $G^{5}/_{6}$, $BG^{4}/_{5}$, $B^{3}/_{4}$,—and is shown graphically in Fig. 12. Its hue sequence is described by the initials YR,Y, GY,G, BG, andB. Its value-sequence appears in the upper numerals, 8, 7, 6, 5, 4, and 3, while the chroma-sequence is included in the lower numerals, 9, 8, 7, 6, 5, and4. This gives a complete statement of the sequence, defining its peculiarity, that at each change of hue there is a regular decrease of value and chroma. Nature seems to be partial to this sequence, constantly reiterating it in yellow flowers with their darker green leaves and underlying shadows. In spring time she may contract its range, making the blue more green and the yellow less red, but in autumn she seems to widen the range, presenting strong contrasts of yellow-red and purple-blue.

(79) Every day she plays upon the values of this sequence, 46 from the strong contrasts of light and shadow at noon to the hardly perceptible differences at twilight. The chroma of this sequence expands during the summer to strong colors, and contracts in winter to grays. Indeed, Nature, who would seem to be the source of our notions of color harmony, rarely repeats herself, yet is endlessly balancing inequalities of hue, value, and chroma by compensations of quantity.

(80) So subtle is this equilibrium that it is taken for granted and forgotten, except when some violent disturbance disarranges it, such as an earthquake or a thunder-storm.

The triple nature of color balance illustrated.

(81) The simplest idea of balance is the equilibrium of two halves of a stick supported at its middle point. If one end is heavier than the other, the support must be moved nearer to that end.

But, since color unites three qualities, we must seek some type of *triple balance*. The game of jackstraws illustrates this, when the disturbance of one piece involves the displacement of two others. The action of three children on a floating plank or the equilibrium of two acrobats carried on the shoulders of a third may also serve as examples.

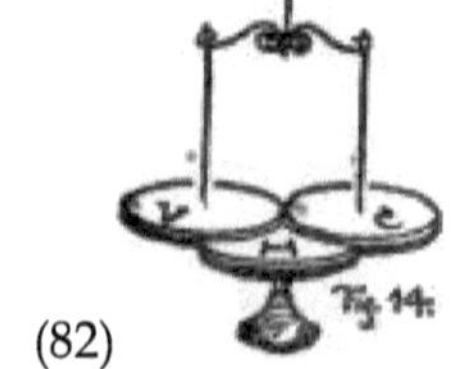

(82) Triple balance may be graphically shown by three discs in contact. Two of them are suspended by their centres,

while they remain in touch with a third supported on a pivot, as in Fig. 14. Let us call the lowest disc Hue (H), and the lateral discs Value (V) and Chroma (C). Any dip or rotation of the lower disc H will induce sympathetic action in the two lateral discs V andC. When H is inclined, both V 47 and C change their relations to it. If H is raised vertically, both V and C dip outward. If H is rotated, both V and C rotate, but in opposite directions. Indeed, any disturbance of V affects H and C, while H and V respond to any movement ofC. So we must be prepared to realize that any change of one color quality involves readjustment of the other two.

(83) Color balance soon leads to a study of optics in one direction, to æsthetics in another, and to mathematical proportions in a third, and any attempt at an easy solution of its problems is not likely to succeed. It is a very complicated question, whose closest counterpart is to be sought in musical rhythms. The fall of musical impulses upon the ear can make us gay or sad, and there are color groups which, acting through the eye, can convey pleasure or pain to the mind.

(84) A colorist is keenly alive to these feelings of satisfaction or annoyance, and consciously or unconsciously he rejects certain combinations of color and accepts others. Successful pictures and decorative schemes are due to some sort of balance uniting "light and shade" (value), "warmth and coolness" (hue), with "brilliancy and grayness" (chroma); for, when they fail to please, the mind at once begins to search for the unbalanced quality, and complains that the color is "too hot," "too dark," or "too crude." This effort to establish pleasing proportions may be unconscious in one temperament, while it becomes a matter of definite analysis in another. Emerson claimed that the unconscious only is complete. We gladly permit those whose color instinct is unerring—(and how few they are!)—to neglect all rules and set formulas. But education is concerned with the many who have not this gift.

(85) Any real progress in color education must come not from a blind imitation of past successes, but by a study into the laws 48 which they exemplify. To exactly copy fine Japanese prints or Persian rugs or Renaissance tapestries, while it cultivates an appreciation of their refinements, does not give one the power to create

things equally beautiful. The masterpieces of music correctly rendered do not of necessity make a composer. The musician, besides the study of masterpieces, absorbs the science of counterpoint, and records by an unmistakable notation the exact character of any new combination of musical intervals which he conceives.

(86) So must the art of the colorist be furnished with a scientific basis and a clear form of color notation. This will record the successes and failures of the past, and aid in a search, by contrast and analysis, for the fundamentals of color balance. Without a measured and systematic notation, attempts to describe color harmony only produce hazy generalities of little value in describing our sensations, and fail to express the essential differences between "good" and "bad" color.

17. Orange is a variable union of yellow and red. See Appendix.

18. Green is often wrongly assigned as the opposite of red. See Appendix, on False Color Balance.

19. Adopted in Course on Optical Measurements at the Massachusetts Institute of Technology. Instruments have also been made for the Harvard Medical School, the Treasury Department in Washington, and various private laboratories.

Appendix to Chapter III.

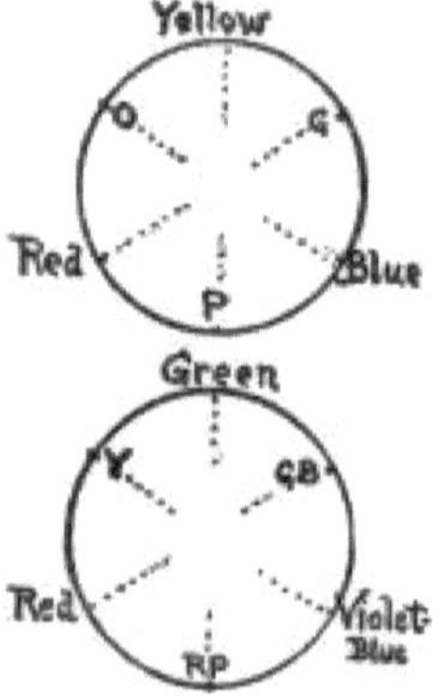

FALSE COLOR BALANCE. There is a widely accepted error that red, yellow, and blue are "primary," although Brewster's theory was long ago dropped when the elements of color vision proved to be RED, GREEN, and VIOLET-BLUE. The late Professor Rood called attention to this in Chapters VIII.–XI. of his book, "Modern Chromatics," which appeared in 1879. Yet we find it very generally taught in school. Nor does the harm end there, for placing red, yellow, and blue equidistant in a circle, with orange, green, and purple as intermediates, the teacher goes on to state that opposite hues are complementary.

Red is	thus made the complement of	Green,
Yellow	" "	Purple, and
Blue	" "	Orange.

Unfortunately, each of these statements is wrong, and, if tested by the mixture of colored lights or with Maxwell's rotating discs, their falsity is evident.

There can be no doubt that green is not the complement of red, nor purple of yellow, nor orange of blue, for neither one of these pairs unites as it should in a balanced neutrality, and a total test of the circle gives great excess of orange, showing that red 50 and yellow usurp too great a portion of the circumference. Starting from a false basis, the Brewster theory can only lead to unbalanced and inharmonious effects of color.

The fundamental color sensations are RED, GREEN, and VIOLET-BLUE.

RED has for its	true complement	BLUE-GREEN,
GREEN	""	RED-PURPLE, and
VIOLET-BLUE	""	YELLOW,

all of the hues in the right-hand column being compound sensations. The sensation of green is not due to a mixture of yellow and blue, as the absorptive action of pigments might lead one to think: GREEN IS FUNDAMENTAL, and not made by mixing any hues of the spectrum, while YELLOW IS NOT FUNDAMENTAL, but caused by the mingled sensations of red and green. This is easily proved by a controlled spectrum, for all yellow-reds, yellows, and green-yellows can be matched by certain proportions of red and green light, all blue-greens, blues, and purple-blues can be obtained by the union of green and violet light, while purple-blue, purple, and red-purple result from the union of violet and red light. But there is no point where a mixture gives red, green, or violet-blue. They are the true primaries, whose mixtures produce all other hues.

Studio and school-room practice still cling to the discredited theory, claiming that, if it fails to describe our color sensations, yet it may be called practically true of pigments, because a red, yellow, and blue pigment suffice to imitate most natural colors. This discrepancy between pigment mixture and retinal mixture becomes clear as soon as one learns the physical make-up and behavior of paints.

51

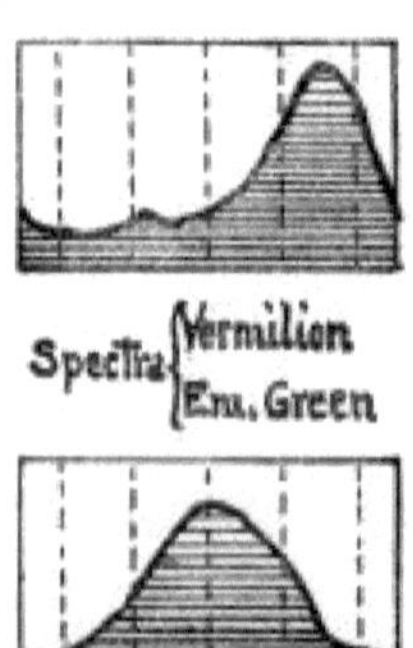

Spectral analysis shows that no pigment is a pure example of the dominant hue which it sends to the eye. Take, for example, the very chromatic pigments representing red and green, such as vermilion and emerald green. If each emitted a single pure hue free from trace of any other hue, then their mixture would appear yellow, as when spectral red and green unite. But, instead of yellow, their mixture produces a warm gray, called brown or "dull salmon," and this is to be inferred from their spectra, where it is seen that vermilion emits some green and purple as well as its dominant color, while the green also sends some blue and red light to the eye.20

Thus stray hues from other parts of the spectrum tend to neutralize the yellow sensation, which would be strong if each of the pigments were pure in the spectral sense. Pigment absorption affects all palette mixtures, and, failing to obtain a satisfactory yellow by mixture of red and green, painters use original yellow pigments,—such as aureolin, cadmium, and lead chromate,—each of them also impure but giving a dominant sensation of yellow. Did the eye discriminate, as does the ear when it analyzes the separate tones of a chord, then we should recognize that yellow pigments emit both red and green rays.

White light dispersed into a colored band by one prism, may have the process reversed by a second prism, so that the eye sees again only white light. But this would not be so, did not the balance of red, green, and violet-blue sensations remain undisturbed. All our ideas of color harmony are based upon this fundamental relation, and, if pigments are to render harmonious effects, 52 we must learn to control their impurities so as to preserve a balance of red, green, and violet-blue.

Otherwise, the excessive chroma and value of red and yellow pigments so overwhelm the lesser degrees of green and blue pigments that no balance is possible, and the colorist of fine perception must reject not alone the theoretical, but also the practical outcome of a "red-yellow-blue" theory.

Some of the points raised in this discussion are rather subtle for students, and may well be left until they arise in a study of optics, but the teacher should grasp them clearly, so as not to be led into false statements about primary and complementary hues.

53

Chapter IV.
PRISMATIC COLOR.

Pure color is seen in the spectrum of sunlight.

(87) The strongest sensation of color is gained in a darkened room, with a prism used to split a beam of sunlight into its various wave lengths. Through a narrow slit there enters a straight pencil of light which we are accustomed to think of as *white,* although it is a bundle of variously colored rays (or waves of ether) whose union and balance is so perfect that no single ray predominates.

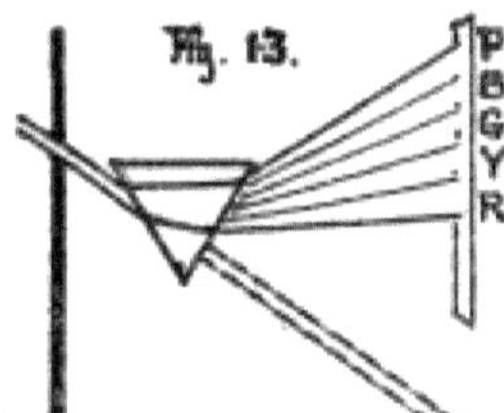

(88) Cover the narrow slit, and we are plunged in darkness. Admit the beam, and the eye feels a powerful contrast between the spot of light on the floor and its surrounding darkness. Place a triangular glass prism near the slit to intercept the beam of white light, and suddenly there appears on the opposite wall a band of brilliant colors. This delightful experiment rivets the eye by the beauty and purity of its hues. All other colors seem weak by comparison.

Their weakness is due to impurity, for all pigments and dyes reflect portions of hues other than their dominant one, which tend to "gray" and diminish their chroma.

(89) But prismatic color is pure, or very nearly so, because the shape of the glass refracts each hue, and separates it by the length 54 of its ether wave. These waves have been measured, and science can name each hue by its wave length. Thus a certain red is known as M. 6867, and a certain green sensation is M. 5269.21 Without attempting any scientific analysis of color, let it be said that Sir Isaac Newton made his series of experiments in 1687, and was privileged to name this color sequence by seven steps which he called red, orange, yellow, green, blue, violet, and indigo. Later a scientist

named Fraunhofer discovered fine black lines crossing the solar spectrum, and marked them with letters of the alphabet from a toh. These with the wave length serve to locate every hue and define every step in the sequence. Since Newton's time it has been proved that only three of the spectral hues are *primary;* viz., ared, agreen, and a violet-blue, while their mixture produces all other gradations. By receiving the spectrum on an opaque screen with fine slits that fit the red and green waves, so that they alone pass through, these two primary hues can be received on mirrors inclined at such an angle as to unite on another screen, where, instead of red or green, the eye sees only yellow.22

(90) A similar arrangement of slits and mirrors for the green and violet-blue proves that they unite to make blue, while a third experiment shows that the red and violet-blue can unite to make purple. So yellow, blue-green, and purple are called secondary 55 hues because they result from the mixture of the three primaries, red, green, and violet-blue.

In comparing these two color lists, we see that the "indigo" and "orange" of Sir Isaac Newton have been discarded. Both are indefinite, and refer to variable products of the vegetable kingdom. Violet is also borrowed from the same kingdom; and, in order to describe a violet, we say it is a purple violet or blue violet, as the case may be, just as we describe an orange as a red orange or a yellow orange. Their color difference is not expressed by the terms "orange" or "violet," but by the words "red," "yellow," "blue," or "purple," all of which are true color names and arouse an unmixed color image.

(91) In the nursery a child learns to use the simple color names red, yellow, green, blue, and purple. When familiarity with the color sphere makes him relate them to each other and place them between black and white by their degree of light and strength, there will be no occasion to revert to vegetables, animals, minerals, or the ever-varying hues of sea and sky to express his color sensations.

(92) Another experiment accentuates the difference between spectral and pigment color. When the spectrum is spread on the screen by the use of a prism, and a second prism is placed inverted beyond the first, it regathers the dispersed rays back into their original beam, making a white spot on the floor. This proves that all the

colored rays of light combine to balance each other in whiteness. But if pigments which are the closest possible imitation of these hues are united on a painter's palette, either by the brush or the knife, they *make gray, and not white.*

(93) This is another illustration of the behavior of pigments, for, instead of uniting to form white, they form gray, which is a 56 darkened or impure form of white; and, lest this should be attributed to a chemical reaction between the various matters that serve as pigments, the experiment can be carried out without allowing one pigment to touch another by using Maxwell discs, as will be shown in the next chapter.

(94) Before leaving these prismatic colors, let us study them in the light of what has already been learned of color dimensions. Not only do they present different values, but also different chromas. Their values range from darkness at each end, where red and purple become visible, to a brightness in the greenish yellow, which is almost white. So on the color tree described in Chapter II., paragraph 34, yellow has the highest branch, green is lower, red is below the middle, with blue and purple lower down, near black.

(95) Then in chroma they range from the powerful stimulation of the red to the soothing purple, with green occupying an intermediate step. This is also given on the color tree by the length of its branches.

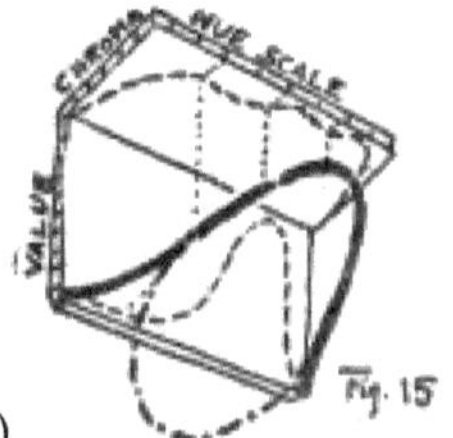

Fig. 15

(96) In Fig. 15 the vertical curve describes the values of the spectrum as they grade from red through yellow, green, blue, and purple. The horizontal curve describes the chromas of the spectrum in the same sequence; while the third curve leaning outward is obtained by uniting the first two by two planes at right angles to one another, and sums up the three qualities by a single descriptive line. Now the red and purple ends are far apart, and science forbids their junction because of their great difference in

wave length. But the mind is prone to unite them in order to produce the red-purples which we see in clouds at sunset, in flowers and 57 grapes and the amethyst. Indeed, it has been done unhesitatingly in most color schemes in order to supply the opposite of green.

(97) This gives a slanting circuit joining all the branch ends of the color tree, and has been likened to the rings of Saturn in ChapterI., paragraph17.

A prismatic color sphere.

(98) With a little effort of the imagination we can picture a prismatic color sphere, using only the colors of light. In a cylindrical chamber is hung a diaphanous ball similar to a huge soap bubble, which can display color on its surface without obscuring its interior. Then, at the proper points of the surrounding wall, three pure beams of colored light are admitted,—one red, another green, and the third violet-blue.

(99) They fall at proper levels on three sides of the sphere, while their intermediate gradations encircle the sphere with a complete spectrum plus the needed purple. As they penetrate the sphere, they unite to balance each other in neutrality. Pure whiteness is at the top, and, by some imaginary means their light gradually diminishes until they disappear in darkness below.

(100) This ideal color system is impossible in the present state of our knowledge and implements. Even were it possible, its immaterial hues could not serve to dye materials or paint pictures. Pigments are, and will in all probability continue to be, the practical agents of coloristic productions, however reluctant the scientist may be to accept them as the basis of a color system. It is true that they are chemically impure and imperfectly represent the colors of light. Some of them fade rapidly and undergo chemical change, as in the notable case of a green pigment tested 58 by this measured system, which in a few weeks lost four steps of chroma, gained two steps of value, and swung into a bluer hue.

(101) But the color sphere to be next described is worked out with a few reliable pigments, mostly natural earths, whose fading is a matter of years and so slight as to be almost imperceptible. Besides,

its principal hues are preserved in safe keeping by imperishable enamels, which can be used to correct any tendency of the pigments to distort the measured intervals of the color sphere.

This meets the most serious objection to a pigment system. Without it a child has nothing tangible which he can keep in constant view to imitate and memorize. With it he builds up a mental image of measured relations that describe every color in nature, including the fleeting hues of the rainbow, although they appear but for a moment at rare intervals. Finally, it furnishes a simple notation which records every color sensation by a letter and two numerals. With the enlargement of his mental power he will unite these in a comprehensive grasp of the larger relations of color.

20. See Rood, Chapter VII., on Color by Absorption.

21. See Micron in Glossary.

22. The fact that the spectral union of red and green makes yellow is a matter of surprise to practical workers in color who are familiar with the action of pigments, but unfamiliar with spectrum analysis. Yellow seems to them a primary and indispensable color, because it cannot be made by the union of red and green pigments. Another surprise is awaiting them when they hear that the yellow and blue of the spectrum make *white*, for all their experience with paints goes to prove that yellow and blue unite to form green. Attention is called to this difference between the mixture of colored light and of colored pigments, not with the idea of explaining it here, but to emphasize their difference; for in the next chapter we shall describe the practical making of a color sphere with pigments, which would be quite impractical, could we have only the colors of the spectrum to work with. See Appendix to preceding chapter.

59

Appendix to Chapter IV.

Children's Color Studies.

These reproductions of children's work are given as proof that color charm and good taste may be cultivated from the start.

FIVE MIDDLE HUES are first taught by the use of special crayons, and later with water colors. They represent the equator of the color sphere (see Plate I.),—a circle midway between the extremes of color-light and color-strength,—and are known as MIDDLE RED, MIDDLE YELLOW, MIDDLE GREEN, MIDDLE BLUE, and MIDDLE PURPLE.

These are starting-points for training the eye to measure regular scales of Value and Chroma.23 Only with such a trained judgment is it safe to undertake the use of strong colors.24

Beginners should avoid Strong Color. Extreme red, yellow, and blue are discordant. (They "shriek" and "swear." Mark Twain calls Roxana's gown "a volcanic eruption of infernal splendors.") Yet there are some who claim that the child craves them, and must have them to produce a thrill. So also does he crave candies, matches, and the carving-knife. He covets the trumpet, fire-gong, and bass-drum for their "thrill"; but who would think them necessary 60 to the musical training of the ear? Like the blazing bill-board and the circus wagon, they may be suffered out-of-doors; but such boisterous sounds and color sprees are unfit for the school-room.

Quiet Color is the Mark of Good Taste. Refinement in dress and the furnishings of the home is attractive, but we shrink from those who are "loud" in their speech or their clothing. If we wish our children to become well-bred, is it logical to begin by encouraging barbarous tastes? Their young minds are very open to suggestion. They quickly adopt our standards, and the blame must fall upon us if they acquire crude color habits. Yellow journalism and rag-time tunes will not help their taste in speech or song, nor will violent hues improve their taste in matters of color.

Balance of Color is to be sought. Artists and decorators are well aware of a fact that slowly dawns upon the student; namely, that color harmony is due to the preservation of a subtle balance and impossible by the use of extremes. This balance of color resides more *within* the spherical surface of this system than in the excessive chromas which project beyond. It is futile to encourage children in efforts to rival the poppy or buttercup, even with the strongest pigments obtainable. Their sunlit points give pleasure because they are surrounded and balanced by blue ether and wide green fields. Were these conditions reversed, so that the flowers appeared as little spots of blue or green in great fields of blazing red, orange, and yellow, our pained eyes would be shut in disgust.

The painter knows that pigments *cannot* rival the brilliancy of the buttercup and poppy, enhanced by their surroundings. What is more, he does not care to attempt it. Nor does the musician wish to imitate the screech of a siren or the explosion of a gun. These are not subjects for art. Harmonious sounds are the study of the musician, and tuned colors are the materials of the colorist. Corot 61 in landscape, and Titian, Velasquez, and Whistler in figure painting, show us that Nature's richest effects and most beautiful color are enveloped in an atmosphere of gray.

Beauty of Color lies in Tempered Relations. Music rarely touches the extreme range of sound, and harmonious color rarely uses the extremes of color-light or color-strength. Regular scales in the middle register are first given to train the ear, and so should the eye be first familiarized with medium degrees of color.

This system provides measured scales, established by special instruments, and is able to select the middle points of red, yellow, green, blue, and purple as a basis for comparing and relating all colors. These five middle colors form a Chromatic Tuning Fork. (See page 70.) It is far better that children should first become familiar with these tuned color intervals which are harmonious in themselves rather than begin by blundering among unrelated degrees of harsh and violent color. Who would think of teaching the musical scale with a piano out of tune?

The Tuning of Color cannot be left to Personal Whim. The wide discrepancies of red, yellow, and blue, which have been falsely taught as primary colors, can no more be tuned by a child than the musical novice can tune his instrument. Each of these hues has three variable factors (see page 14, paragraph 14), and scientific tests are necessary to measure and relate their uneven degrees of Hue, Value, and Chroma.

Visual estimates of color, without the help of any standard for comparison, are continually distorted by doubt, guess-work, and the fatigue of the eye. Hardly two persons can agree in the intelligible description of color. Not only do individuals differ, but the same eye will vary in its estimates from day to day. Afrequent assumption that all strong pigments are equal in chroma, is 62 far from the truth, and involves beginners in many mishaps. Thus the strongest blue-green, chromium sesquioxide, is but half the chroma of its red complement, the sulphuret of mercury. Yet ignorance is constantly leading to their unbalanced use. Indeed, some are still unaware that they are the complements of each other.25

It is evident that the fundamental scales of Hue, Value, and Chroma must be established by scientific measures, not by personal bias. This system is unique in the possession of such scales, made possible by the devising of special instruments for the measurement of color, and can therefore be trusted as a permanent basis for training the color sense.

The examples in Plates II. and III. show how successfully the tuned crayons, cards, and water colors of this system lead a child to fine appreciations of color harmony.

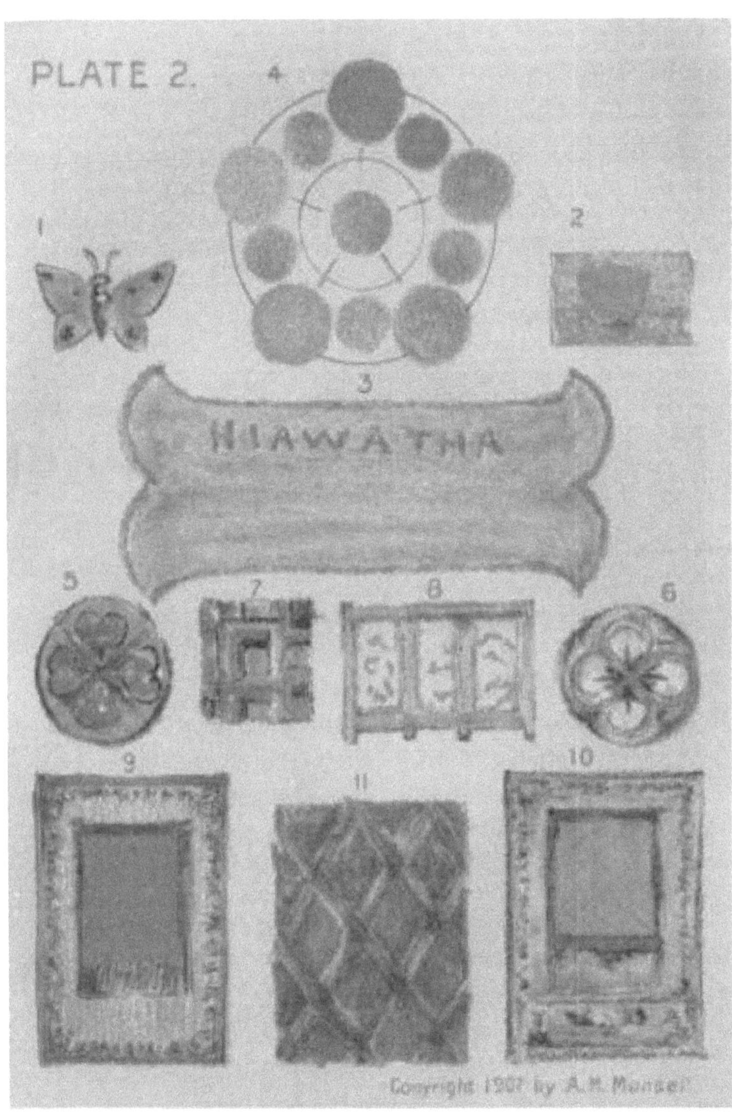
PLATE 2.
4
1
2
3
HIAWATHA
5
7
8
6
9
11
10

PLATE II.
Color Studies with TUNED CRAYONS in the Lower Grades.

Children have made every example on this plate, with no other material than the five crayons of middle hue, tempered with gray and black. AColor Sphere is always kept in the room for reference, and five color balls to match the five middle hues are placed in the hands of the youngest pupils. Starting with these middle points in the scales of Value and Chroma, they learn to estimate rightly all lighter and darker values, all weaker and stronger chromas, and gradually build up a disciplined judgment of color.

63

Each study can be made the basis of many variations by a simple change of one color element, as suggested in the text.

1. Butterfly. Yellow and black crayon. Vary by using any single crayon with black.

2. Dish. Red crayon, blue and green crayons for back and foreground. Vary by using the two opposites of any color chosen for the dish and omitting the two neighboring colors. See No.4.

3. Hiawatha's canoe. Yellow crayon, with rim and name in green. Vary color of canoe, keeping the rim a neighboring color. See No.4.

4. Color-circle. Gray crayon for centre, and five crayons spaced equidistant. This gives the invariable order, red, yellow, green, blue, purple. *Never use all five in a single design.* Either use a color and its two neighbors or a color and its two opposites. By mingling touches of any two neighbors, the intermediates are made and named yellow-red (orange), green-yellow, blue-green, purple-blue (violet), and red-purple. Abbreviated, the circle reads R, YR, Y, GY, G, BG, B, PB, P,RP.

5. Rosette. Red cross in centre, green leaves: blue field, black outline. Vary as in No.2.

6. Rosette. Green centre and edge of leaves, purple field and black accents. Vary color of centre, keeping field two colors distant.

7. Plaid. Use any three crayons with black. Vary the trio.

8. Folding screen. Yellow field (lightly applied), green and black edge. Make lighter and darker values of each color, and arrange in scales graded from black to white.

9. Rug. Light red field with solid red centre, border pattern and edges of gray. This is called self-color. Change to each of the crayons.

64

10. Rug. Light yellow field and solid centre, with purple and black in border design. Vary by change of ground, keeping design two colors distant and darkened with black.

11. Lattice. Yellow with black: alternate green and blue lozenges. Vary by keeping the lozenges of two neighboring colors, but one color removed from that of the lattice.

For principles involved in these color groups, see Chapter III.

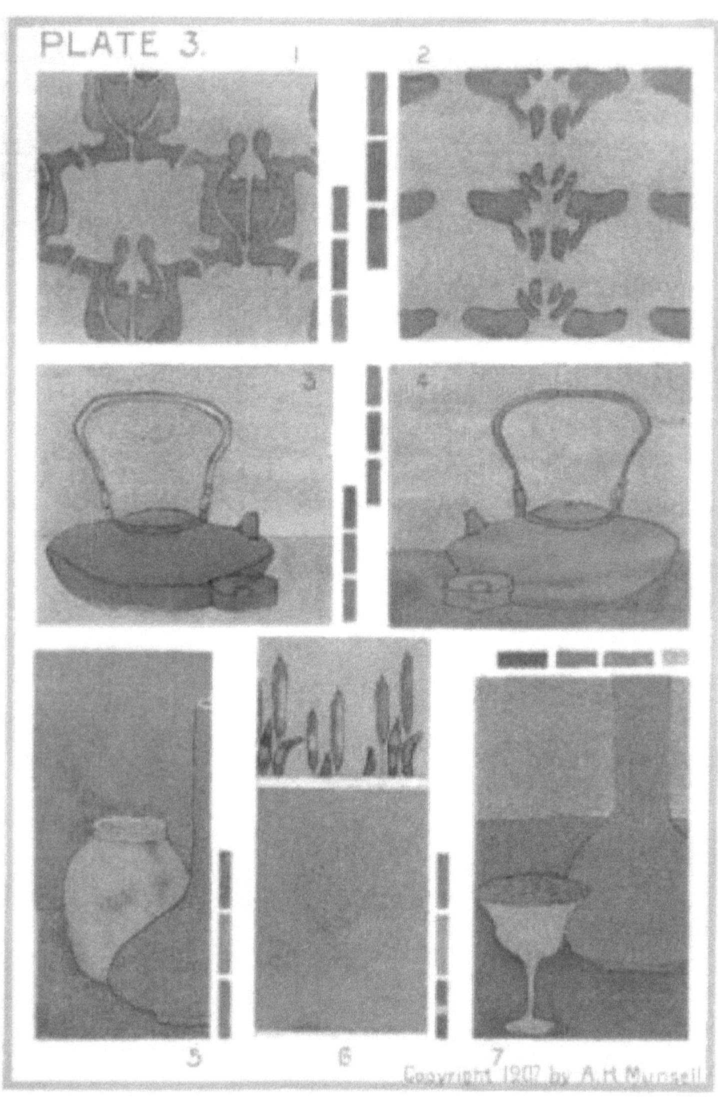
PLATE 3.
1
2
3
4
5
6
7
Copyright 1907 by A.H.Munsell

PLATE III.
Color Studies with TUNED WATER COLORS in the Upper Grades.

Previous work with measured scales, made by the tuned crayons and tested by reference to the color sphere, have so trained the color judgment that children may now be trusted with more flexible material. They have memorized the equable degrees of color on the equator of the sphere, and found how lighter colors may balance darker colors, how small areas of stronger chroma may be balanced by larger masses of weaker chroma, and in general gained a disciplined color sense. Definite impressions and clear thinking have taken the place of guess-work and blundering.

Thus, before reaching the secondary school, they are put in possession of the color faculty by a system and notation similar to that which was devised centuries ago for the musical sense. No system, however logical, will produce the artist, but every artist needs some systematic training at the outset, and this simple method by measured scales is believed to be the best yet devised.

Each example on this plate may be made the basis of many variants, by small changes in the color steps, as suggested in the 65 text, and further elaborated in Chapter VI. Indeed, the studies reproduced on Plates II. and III. are but a handful among hundreds of pleasing results produced in a single school.26

1. Pattern. Purple and green: the two united and thinned with water will give the ground. Vary with any other color pair.

2. Pattern. Figure in middle red, with darker blue-green accent. Ground of middle yellow, grayed with slight addition of the red and green. Vary with purple in place of blue-green.

3. Japanese teapot. Middle red, with background of lighter yellow and foreground of grayed middle yellow.

4. Variant on No. 3. Middle yellow, with slight addition of green. Foreground the same, with more red, and background of middle gray.

5. Group. Background of yellow-red, lighter vase in yellow-green, and darker vase of green, with slight addition of black. Vary by inversion of the colors in ground and darker vase.

6. Wall decoration. Frieze pattern made of cat-tails and leaves,—the leaves of blue-green with black, tails of yellow-red with black, and ground of the two colors united and thinned with water. Wall of blue-green, slightly grayed by additions of the two colors in the frieze. Dado could be a match of the cat-tails slightly grayer. *See Fig. 23, page 82.*

7. Group. Foreground in purple-blue, grayed with black. Vase of purple-red, and background in lighter yellow-red, grayed.

For analysis of the groups and means of recording them, see Chapter III.

23. See Century Dictionary for definition of chroma. Under the word "color" will be found definitions of Primary, Complementary, Constants (chroma, luminosity, and hue), and the Young-Helmholtz theory of color-sensation.

24. It must not be assumed because so much stress is laid upon quiet and harmonious color that this system excludes the more powerful degrees. To do so would forfeit its claim to completeness. AColor Atlas in preparation displays all known degrees of pigment color arranged in measured scales of Hue, Value, and Chroma.

25. See Appendix to Chapter III.

26. The Pope School, Somerville, Mass.

66

Chapter V.
A PIGMENT COLOR SPHERE.27

How to make a color sphere with pigments.

(102) The preceding chapters have built up an ideal color solid, in which every sensation of color finds its place and is clearly named by its degree of hue, value, and chroma.

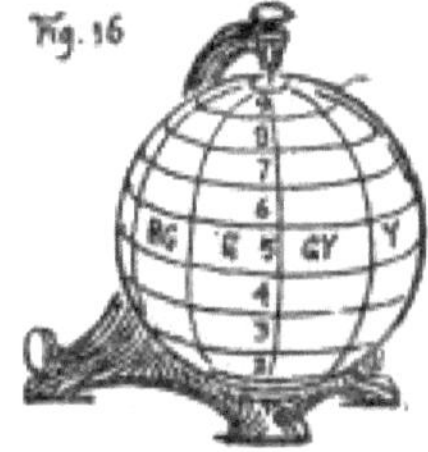

It has been shown that the neutral centre of the system is a balancing point for all colors, that a line through this centre finds opposite colors which balance and complement each other; and we are now ready to make a practical application, carrying out these ideal relations of color as far as pigments will permit in a color sphere27 (Fig.16).

(103) The materials are quite simple. First a colorless globe, mounted so as to spin freely on its axis. Then a measured scale of value, specially devised for this purpose, obtained by the daylight photometer.28 Next a set of carefully chosen pigments, whose reasonable permanence has been tested by long use, and which are prepared so that they will not glisten when spread on the surface of the globe, but give a uniformly mat surface. Aglass palette, palette knife, and some fine brushes complete the list.

(104) Here is a list of the paints arranged in pairs to represent 67 the five sets of opposite hues described in Chapter III., paragraphs 61-63: –

Color Pairs.	*Pigments Used.*	*Chemical Nature.*
Red and	Venetian red.	Calcined native earth.

Blue-green.	Viridian and Cobalt.	Chromium sesquioxide.
Yellow and	Raw Sienna.	Native earth.
Purple-blue.	Ultramarine.	Artificial product.
Green and	Emerald green.	Arsenate of copper.
Red-purple.	Purple madder.	Extract of the madder plant.
Blue and	Cobalt.	Oxide of cobalt with alumina.
Yellow-red.	Orange cadmium.	Sulphide of cadmium.
Purple and	Madder and cobalt.	See each pigment above.
Green-yellow.	Emerald green and Sienna.	See each pigment above.

(105) These paints have various degrees of hue, value, and chroma, but can be tempered by additions of the neutrals, zinc white and ivory black, until each is brought to a middle value and tested on the value scale. After each pair has been thus balanced, they are painted in their appropriate spaces on the globe, forming an equator of balanced hues.

(106) The method of proving this balance has already been suggested in Chapter IV., paragraph 93. It consists of an ingenious implement devised by Clerk-Maxwell, which gives us a result of mixing colors without the chemical risks of letting them come in contact, and also measures accurately the quantity of each which is used (Fig.17).

(107) This is called a Maxwell disc, and is nothing more than 68 a circle of firm cardboard, pierced with a central hole to fit the spindle of a rotary motor, and with a radial slit from rim to centre, so that

another disc may be slid over the first to cover any desired fraction of its surface. Let us paint one of these discs with Venetian red and the other with viridian and cobalt, the first pair in the list of pigments to be used on the globe.

(108) Having dried these two discs, one is combined with the other on the motor shaft so that each color occupies half the circle. As soon as the motor starts, the two colors are no longer distinguished, and rapid rotation melts them so perfectly that the eye sees a new color, due to their mixture on the retina. This new color is a reddish gray, showing that the red is more chromatic than the blue-green. But by stopping the motor and sliding the green disc to cover more of the red one, there comes a point where rotation melts them into a perfectly neutral gray. No hint of either hue remains, and the pair is said to balance.

(109) Since this balance has been obtained by *unequal areas* of the two pigments, it must compensate for a lack of equal chroma in the hues (see paragraphs 76, 77); and, to measure this inequality, aslightly larger disc, with decimal divisions on its rim, is placed back of the two painted ones. If this scale shows the red as occupying $3\frac{1}{3}$ parts of the area, while blue-green occupies $6\frac{2}{3}$ parts, then the blue-green must be only half as chromatic as the red, since it takes twice as much to produce the balance.

(110) The red is then grayed (diminished in chroma by additions of a middle gray) until it can occupy half the circle, with blue-green on the remaining half, and still produce neutrality when mixed by rotation. Each disc now reads 5 on the decimal scale. Lest the graying of red should have disturbed its value, it is again tested on the photometric scale, and reads 4.7, showing it has been 69 slightly darkened by the graying process. Alittle white is therefore added until its value is restored to5.

(111) The two opposites are now completely balanced, for they are equal in value (5), equal in chroma (5), and have proved their equality as complements by uniting in equal areas to form a neutral mixture. It only remains to apply them in their proper position on the sphere.

(112) A band is traced around the equator, divided in ten equal spaces, and lettered R, YR, Y, GY, G, BG, B, PB, P, and RP (see Fig.

18). This balanced red and blue-green are applied with the brush to spaces marked R and BG, care being taken to fill, but not to overstep the bounds, and the color laid absolutely flat, that no unevenness of value or chroma may disturb the balance.

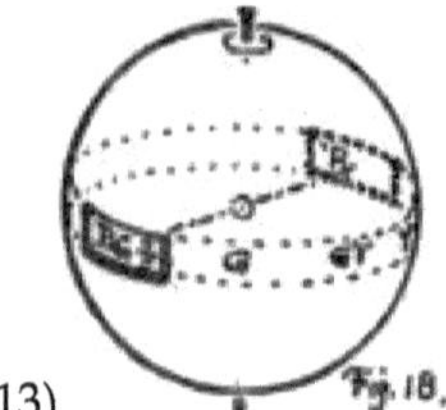

Fig. 18.

(113) The next pair, represented by Raw Sienna and Ultramarine, is similarly brought to middle value, balanced by equal areas on the Maxwell discs, and, when correct in each quality, is painted in the spaces Y and PB. Emerald Green and Purple Madder, which form the next pigment pair, are similarly tempered, proved, and applied, followed by the two remaining pairs, until the equator of the globe presents its ten equal steps of middle hues.

An equator of ten balanced hues.

(114) Now comes the total test of this circuit of balanced hues by rotation of the sphere. As it gains speed, the colors flash less and less, and finally melt into a middle gray of perfect neutrality. Had it failed to produce this gray and shown a tinge of any hue still persisting, we should say that the persistent hue was in excess, or, conversely, that its opposite hue was deficient in chroma, and failed to preserve its share in the balance.

(115) For instance, had rotation discovered the persistence of reddish gray, it would have proved the red too strong, or its opposite, blue-green, too weak, and we should have been forced to retrace our steps, applying a correction until neutrality was established by the rotation test.

(116) This is the practical demonstration of the assertion (ChapterI., paragraph8) that a *color has three dimensions which can be measured.* Each of these ten middle hues has proved its right to a definite place on the color globe by its measurements of value and chroma. Being of equal chroma, all are equidistant from the neutral centre,

and, being equal in value, all are equally removed from the poles. If the warm hues (red and yellow) or the cool hues (blue and green) were in excess, the rotation test of the sphere would fail to produce grayness, and so detect its lack of balance.29

A chromatic tuning fork.

(117) The five principal steps in this color equator are made in permanent enamel and carefully safeguarded, so that, if the pigments painted on the globe should change or become soiled, it could be at once detected and set right. These five are middle red (so called because midway between white and black, as well as midway between our strongest red and the neutral centre), middle yellow, middle green, middle blue, and middle purple. They may be called the CHROMATIC TUNING FORK, for they serve to establish the pitch of colors, as the musical tuning fork preserves the pitch of sounds.

Completion of a pigment color sphere.

(118) When the chromatic tuning fork has thus been obtained, 71 the completion of the globe is only a matter of patience, for the same method can be applied at any level in the scale of value, and a new circuit of balanced hues made to conform with its position between the poles of white and black.

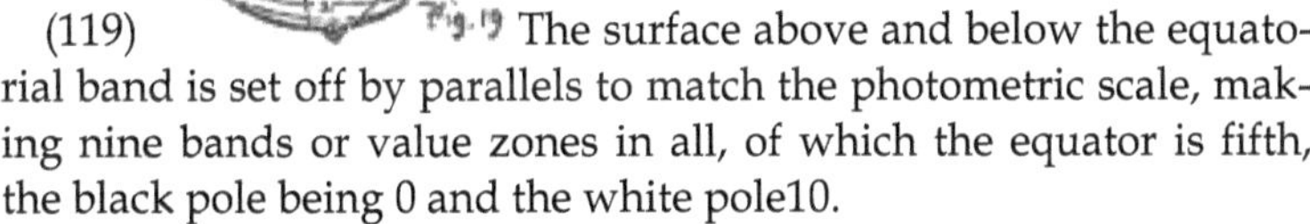

(119) Fig. 19 The surface above and below the equatorial band is set off by parallels to match the photometric scale, making nine bands or value zones in all, of which the equator is fifth, the black pole being 0 and the white pole10.

(120) Ten meridians carry the equatorial hues across all these value zones and trace the gradation of each hue through a complete scale from black to white, marked by their values, as shown in paragraph 68. Thus the red scale is R^1, R^2, R^3, R^4, R^5 (middle red), R^6, R^7, R^8, and R^9, and similarly with each of the other hues. When the cir-

cle of hues corresponding to each level has been applied and tested, the entire surface of the globe is spread with a logical system of color scales, and the eye gratified with regular sequences which move by measured steps in each direction.

(121) Each meridian traces a scale of value for the hue in which it lies. Each parallel traces a scale of hue for the value at whose level it is drawn. Any oblique path across these scales traces a regular sequence, each step combining change of hue with a change of value and chroma. The more this path approaches the vertical, the less are its changes of hue and the more its changes of value and chroma; while, the nearer it comes to the horizontal, the less are its changes of value and chroma, while the greater become its changes of hue. Of these two oblique paths the first may be called that of a Luminist, or painter like Rembrandt, whose canvases present great contrasts of light and shade, while the second 72 is that of the Colorist, such as Titian, whose work shows great fulness of hues without the violent extremes of white and black.

Total balance of the sphere tested by rotation on any desired axis.

(122) Not only does the mount of the color sphere permit its rotation on the vertical axis (white-black), but it is so hung that it may be spun on the ends of any desired axis, as, for instance, that joining our first color pair, red and blue-green. With this pair as poles of rotation, anew equator is traced through all the values of purple on one side and of green-yellow on the other, which the rotation test melts in a perfect balance of middle gray, proving the correctness of these values. In the same way it may be hung and tested on successive axes, until the total balance of the entire spherical series is proved.

(123) But this color system does not cease with the colors spread on the surface of a globe.[30] The first illustration of an orange filled with color was chosen for the purpose of stimulating the imagination to follow a surface color inward to the neutral axis by regular decrease of chroma. Aslice at any level of the solid, as at value 8 (Fig. 10), shows each hue of that level passing by even steps of increasing grayness to the neutral gray N^8 of the axis. In the case of red at this level, it is easily described by the notation $R^8/_3$, $R^8/_2$,

$R^{8}/_{1}$, of which the initial and upper numerals do not change, but the lower numeral traces loss of chroma by 3, 2, and 1 to the neutral axis.

(124) And there are stronger chromas of red outside the surface, which can be written $R^{8}/_{4}$, $R^{8}/_{5}$, $R^{8}/_{6}$, etc. Indeed, our color measurements discover such differences of chroma in the various pigments used, that the color tree referred to in paragraphs 34, 35, is necessary 73 to bring before the eye their maximum chromas, most of which are well outside the spherical shell and at various levels of value. One way to describe the color sphere is to suggest that a color tree, the intervals between whose irregular branches are filled with appropriate color, can be placed in a turning lathe and turned down until the color maxima are removed, thus producing a color solid no larger than the chroma of its weakest pigment (Fig.2).

Charts of the color solid.

(125) Thus it becomes evident that, while the color sphere is a valuable help to the child in conceiving color relations, in uniting the three scales of color measure, and in furnishing with its mount an excellent test of the theory of color balance, yet it is always restricted to the chroma of its weakest color, the surplus chromas of all other colors being thought of as enormous mountains built out at various levels to reach the maxima of our pigments.

(126) The complete color solid is, therefore, of irregular shape, with mountains and valleys, corresponding to the inequalities of pigments. To display these inequalities to the eye, we must prepare cross sections or charts of the solid, some horizontal, some vertical, and others oblique.

(127) Such a set of charts forms an atlas of the color solid, enabling one to see any color in its relation to all other colors, and name it by its degree of hue, value, and chroma. Fig. 20 is a horizontal chart of all colors which present middle value (5), and describes by an uneven contour the chroma of every hue at this level. The dotted fifth circle is the equator of the color sphere, whose principal hues, $R^{5}/_{5}$. $Y^{5}/_{5}$, $G^{5}/_{5}$, $B^{5}/_{5}$, and $P^{5}/_{5}$, form the chromatic tuning fork, paragraph 117.

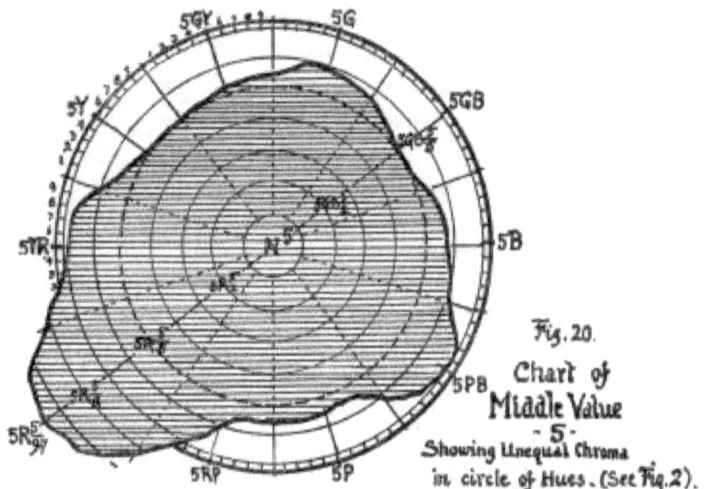

Fig. 20. Chart of Middle Value -5- Showing Unequal Chroma in circle of Hues. (See Fig. 2).

(128) In this single chart the eye readily distinguishes some three hundred different colors, each of which may be written by its hue, value, and chroma. And even the slightest variation of one of them can be defined. Thus, if the principal red were to fade slightly, so that it was a trifle lighter and a trifle weaker than the enamel, it would be written $R^{5.1}/_{4.9}$, showing it had lightened by 1 per cent. and weakened by 1 per cent. The discrimination made possible by this decimal notation is much finer than our present visual limit. Its use will stimulate finer perception of color.

(129) Such a very elementary sketch of the Color Solid and Color Atlas, which is all that can be given in the confines of this small book, will be elsewhere presented on a larger and more complete scale. It should be contrasted with the ideal form composed of prismatic colors, suggested in the last chapter, paragraphs 7598, 99, which was shown to be impracticable, but whose ideal conditions it follows as far as the limitations of pigments permit.

(130) Besides its value in education as setting all our color notions in order, and supplying a simple method for their clear expression, it promises to do away with much of the misunderstanding that accompanies the every-day use of color.

(131) Popular color names are incongruous, irrational, and often ludicrous. One must smile in reading the list of 25 steps in a scale of blue, made by Schiffer-Muller in 1772: —

A.	*a.*	White pure.
	b.	White silvery or pearly.
	c.	White milky.
B.	*a.*	Bluish white.
	b.	Pearly white.
	c.	Watery white.
C.		Blue being born.
D.		Blue dying or pale.
E.		Mignon blue.
F.		Celestial blue, or sky-color.
G.	*a.*	Azure, or ultramarine.
	b.	Complete or perfect blue.
	c.	Fine or queen blue.
H.		Covert blue or turquoise.
I.		King blue (deep).
J.		Light brown blue or indigo.
K.	*a.*	Persian blue or woad flower.
	b.	Forge or steel blue.
	c.	Livid blue.
L.	*a.*	Blackish blue.
	b.	Hellish blue.
	c.	Black-blue.
M.	*a.*	Blue-black or charcoal.
	b.	Velvet black.
	c.	Jet black.

The advantage of spacing these 25 colors in 13 groups, some with three and others with but one example, is not apparent; nor why ultramarine should be several steps above turquoise, for the reverse is generally true. Besides which the hue of turquoise is greenish, while that of ultramarine is purplish, but the list cannot show this; and the remarkable statement that one kind of blue is "hellish," while another is "celestial," should rest upon an experience that few can claim. Failing to define color-value and color-hue, the list gives no hint of color-strength, except at 76 C and D, where one kind of blue is "dying" when the next is "being born," which not inaptly describes the color memory of many a person. Finally, it assures us that Queen blue is "fine" and King blue is "deep."

This year the fashionable shades are "burnt onion" and "fresh spinach." The florists talk of a "pink violet" and a "green pink." Amaker of inks describes the red as a "true crimson scarlet," which is a contradiction in terms. These and a host of other names borrowed from the most heterogeneous sources, become outlawed as soon as the simple color terms and measures of this system are adopted.

Color anarchy is replaced by systematic color description.

27. Patented Jan. 9, 1900.

28. See paragraph 65.

29. Such a test would have exposed the excess of warm color in the schemes of Runge and Chevreul, as shown in the Appendix to this chapter.

30. No color is excluded from this system, but the excess and inequalities of pigment chroma are traced in the Color Atlas.

77

Appendix to Chapter V.

Color schemes based on Brewster's mistaken theory.

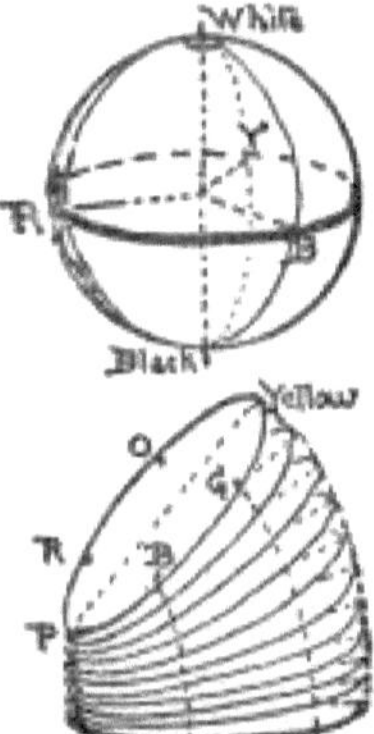

Runge, of Hamburg (1810), suggested that red, yellow, and blue be placed equidistant around the equator of a sphere, with white and black at opposite poles. As the yellow was very light and the blue very dark, any coherency in the value scales of red, yellow, and blue was impossible.

Chevreul, of Paris (1861), seeking uniform color scales for his workmen at the Gobelins, devised a hollow cylinder built up of ten color circles. The upper circle had red, yellow, and blue spaced equidistant, and, as in Runge's solid, yellow was very light and blue very dark. Each circle was then made "one-tenth" darker than the next above, until black was reached at the base. Although each circle was supposed to lie horizontally, only the black lowest circle presents a level of uniform values.

Yellow values increase their luminosity thrice as fast as purple values, so that each circle should tilt at an increasing angle, and the upper circle of strongest colors be inclined at 60° to the black base. Besides this fault shared with Runge's sphere, it falls into another by not diminishing the size of the lower circles where added black diminishes the chroma.

Desire to make colors fit a chosen contour, and the absence of 78 measuring instruments, cause these schemes to ignore the facts of color relation. Like ancient maps made to satisfy a conqueror, they amuse by their distortion.

Brewster's mistaken theory underlies these schemes, as is also the case with Froebel's gifts, whose color balls continue to give wrong notions at the very threshold of color education. As pointed out in the Appendix to Chapter III., the "red-yellow-blue" theory inevitably spreads the warm field of yellow-red too far, and contracts the blue field, so that balance of color is rendered impossible, as illustrated in the gaudy chromo and flaming bill-board.

These schemes are criticised by Rood as "not only in the main arbitrary, but also vague"; and, although Chevreul's charts were published by the government in most elaborate form, their usefulness is small. Interest in the growth of the present system, because of its measured character, led Professor Rood to give assistance in the tests, and at his request a color sphere was made for the Physical Cabinet at Columbia.

Chapter VI.
COLOR NOTATION.

Suggestion of a chromatic score.

(132) The last chapter traced a series of steps leading to the construction of a practical color sphere. Each color was tested by appropriate instruments to assure its degree of hue, value, and chroma, before being placed in position. Then the total sphere was tested to detect any lack of balance.

(133) Each color was also *written* by a letter and two numerals, showing its place in the three scales of hue, value, and chroma. This naturally suggests, not only a record of each separate color sensation, but also a union of these records in series and groups to form a *color score*, similar to the musical score by which the measured relations of sound are recorded.

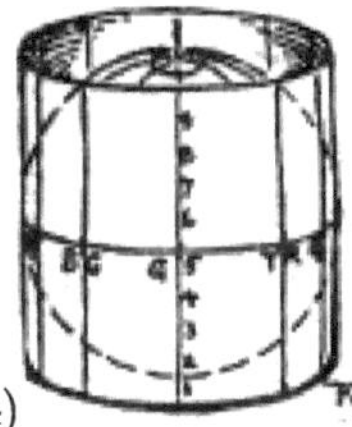

(134) A very simple form of color score may be easily imagined as a transparent envelope wrapped around the equator of the sphere, and forming a vertical cylinder (Fig. 21). On the envelope the equator traces a horizontal centre line, which is at 5 of the *value scale*, with zones 6, 7, 8, and 9 as parallels above, and the zones 4, 3, 2, and 1 below. Vertical lines are drawn through ten equidistant points on this centre line, corresponding with the divisions of the *hue scale*, and marked R, YR, Y, GY, G, BG, B, PB, P, andRP.

80

(135) The transparent envelope is thus divided into one hundred compartments, which provide for ten steps of value in each of the ten middle colors. Now, if we cut open this envelope along one of the verticals,—as, for instance, red-purple (RP), it may be spread out, making a flat chart of the color sphere (Fig.22).

Why green is given the centre of the score.

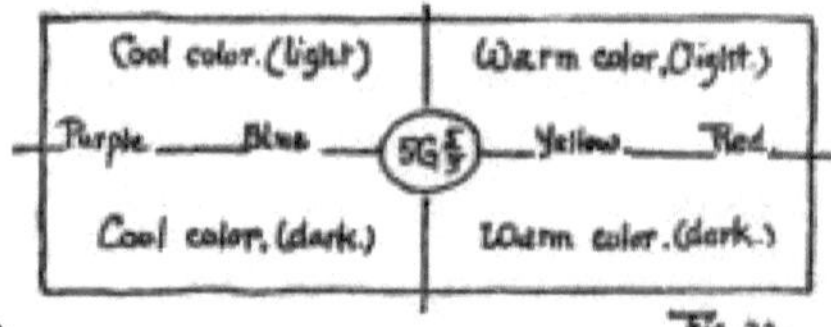

Fig. 22.

(136) A cylindrical envelope might be opened on any desired meridian, but it is an advantage to have green (G) at the centre of the chart, and it is therefore opened at the opposite point, red-purple (RP). To the right of the green centre are the meridians of green-yellow (GY), yellow (Y), yellow-red (YR), and red (R), all of which are known as *warm colors*, because they contain yellow and red. To the left are the meridians of blue-green (BG), blue (B), purple-blue (PB), and purple (P), all of which are called *cool colors*, because they contain blue. Green, being neither warm nor cold of itself, and becoming so only by additions of yellow or of blue, thus serves as a balancing point or centre in the hue-scale.31

(137) The color score presents four large divisions or color fields made by the intersection of the equator with the meridian of green. Above the centre are all light colors, and below it are all dark colors. To the right of the centre are all warm colors, and to the left are all cool colors. Middle green ($5G^5/_5$) is the centre of balance for these contrasted qualities, recognized by all 81 practical color workers. The chart forms a rectangle whose length equals the equator of the color sphere and its height equals the axis (aproportion of 3.14:1), representing a union and balance of the scales of hue and of value. This provides for two color dimensions; but, to be complete, the chart must provide for the third dimension, chroma.

(138) Replacing the chart around the sphere and joining its ends, so that it re-forms the transparent envelope, we may thrust a pin through at any point until it pierces the surface of the sphere. Indeed, the pin can be thrust deeper until it reaches the neutral axis, thus forming a scale of chroma for the color point where it enters (see paragraph 12). In the same way any colors on the sphere, within the sphere, or without it, can have pins thrust into the chart to mark their place, and the length by which each pin projects can be taken as a measure of chroma. If the chart is now unrolled, it retains

the pins, which by their place describe the hue and value of a color, while their length describes its chroma.

Pins stuck into the score represent chroma.

(139) With this idea of the third color dimension incorporated in the score we can discard the pin, and record its length by a numeral. Any dot placed on the score marks a certain degree of hue and value, while a numeral beside it marks the degree of chroma which it carries, uniting with the hue and value of that point to give us a certain color. Glancing over a series of such color points, the eye easily grasps their individual character, and connects them into an intelligible series.

(140) Thus a flat chart becomes the projection of the color solid, and any color in that solid is transferred to the surface of the chart, retaining its degrees of hue, value, and chroma. So far the scales have been spoken of as divided into ten steps, but 82 they may be subdivided much finer, if desired, by use of the decimal point. It is a question of convenience whether to make a small score with only the large divisions, or a much larger score with a hundred times as many steps. In the latter case each hue has ten steps, the middle step of green being distinguished as $5G^{5}/_{5}$ to suggest the four steps 1G, 2G, 3G, 4G, which precede it, and 6G, 7G, 8G, and 9G, which follow it toward blue-green.

Fig 23.

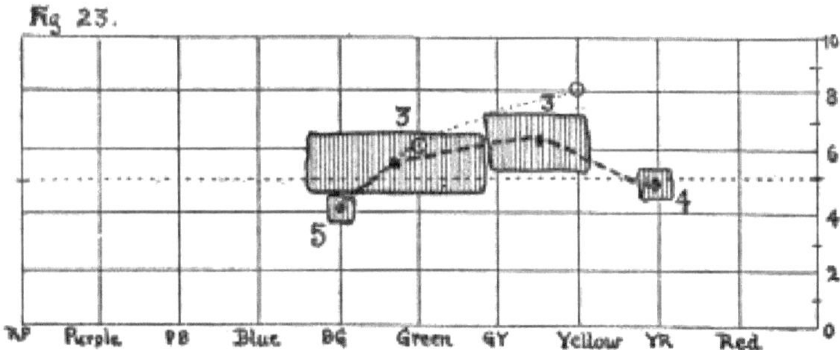

The score preserves color records in a convenient shape.

Such a color score, or notation diagram, to be made small or large as the case demands, offers a very convenient means for recording color combinations, when pigments are not at hand.

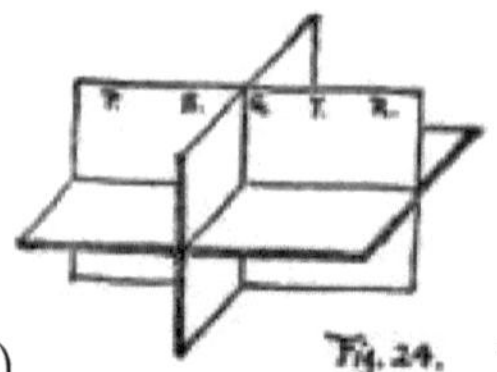
Fig. 24.

(141) To display its three dimensions, a little model can be made with three visiting cards, so placed as to present their mutual intersection at right angles (Fig.24).

$5G\ ^5/_5$ is their centre of mutual balance. Acentral plane separates all colors into two contrasted fields. To the right are all warm colors, to the left are all cool colors. Each of these 83 fields is again divided by the plane of the equator into lighter colors above and darker colors below. These four color fields are again subdivided by a transverse plane through $5G^5/_5$ into strong colors in front and weak colors beyond or behindit.

(142) Any color group, whose record must all be written to the right of the centre, is warm, because red and yellow are dominant. One to the left of the centre must be cool, because it is dominated by blue. Agroup written all above the centre must have light in excess, while one written entirely below is dark to excess. Finally, ascore written all in front of the centre represents only strong chromas, while one written behind it contains only weak chromas. From this we gather that a balanced composition of color preserves some sort of equilibrium, uniting degrees of warm and cool, of light and dark, and of weak and strong, which is made at once apparent by the dots on the score.

(143) A single color, like that of a violet, arose, or a buttercup, appears as a dot on the score, with a numeral added for its chroma. Aparti-colored flower, such as a nasturtium, is shown by two dots with their chromas, and a bunch of red and yellow flowers will give by their dots a color passage, or "silhouette," whose warmth and lightness is unmistakable.

The chroma of each flower written with the silhouette completes the record. The hues of a beautiful Persian rug, with dark red predominating, or a verdure tapestry, in which green is dominant, or a Japanese print, with blue dominant, will trace upon the score a pattern descriptive of its color qualities. These records, with practice, become as significant to the eye as the musical score. The general character of a color combination is apparent at a glance, while its degrees of chroma are readily joined to fill out the mental image.

84

(144) Such a plan of color notation grows naturally from the spherical system of measured colors. It is hardly to be hoped, in devising a color score, that it should not seem crude at first. But the measures forming the basis of this record can be verified by impartial instruments, and have a permanent value in the general study of color. They also afford some definite data as to personal bias in color estimates.

(145) This makes it possible to collect in a convenient form two contrasting and valuable records, one preserving such effects of color as are generally called pleasing, and another of such groups as are found unpleasant to the eye. Out of such material something may be gained, more reliable than the shifting, personal, and contradictory statements about color harmony now prevalent.

31. To put this in terms of the spectrum wave lengths, long waves at the red end of the spectrum give the sensation of warmth, while short waves at the violet end cause the sensation of coolness. Midway between these extremes is the wave length of green.

85

Chapter VII.
COLOR HARMONY.

Colors may be grouped to please or to give annoyance.

(146) Attempts to define the laws of harmonious color have not attained marked success, and the cause is not far to seek. The very sensations underlying these effects of concord or of discord are themselves undefined. The misleading formula of my student days—that three parts of yellow, five parts of red, and eight parts of blue would combine harmoniously—was unable to define the *kind* of red, yellow, and blue intended; that is, the hue, value, and chroma of each of these colors was unknown, and the formula meant a different thing to each person who tried to useit.

(147) It is true that a certain red, green, and blue can be united in such proportions on Maxwell discs as to balance in a neutral gray; but the slightest change in either the hue, value, or chroma, of any one of them, upsets the balance. Anew proportion is then needed to regain the neutral mixture. This has already been shown in the discussion of triple balance (paragraph82).

(148) Harmony of color has been still further complicated by the use of terms that belong to musical harmony. Now music is a *measured art,* and has found a set of intervals which are defined scientifically. The two arts have many points of similarity; and the impulses of sound waves on the ear, like those of light waves on the eye, are measured vibrations. But they are far apart in their scales, and differ so much in important 86 particulars that no practical relationship can be set up. The intervals of color sensation require fit names and measures, ere their infinite variety can be organized into a fixed system.

(149) Any effort to compare certain sounds to certain colors soon leads to the wildest vagaries.

Harmony of sound is unlike harmony of color.

(150) The poverty of color language tempts to a borrowing from the richer terminology of music. Musical terms, such as "pitch, key, note, tone, chord, modulation, nocturne, and symphony," are fre-

quently used in the description of color, serving by association to convey certain vague ideas.

(151) In the same way the term *color harmony,* from association with musical harmony, presents to the mind an image of color arrangement,—varied, yet well proportioned, grouped in orderly fashion, and agreeable to the eye. But any attempt to define this image in terms of color is disappointing. Here is a beautiful Persian rug: why do we call it beautiful? One says "because its colors are *rich.*" Why are they rich? "Because they are *deep in tone.*" What does that mean? The double-bass and the fog-horn are *deep* in tone, but not necessarily beautiful on that account. "Oh, no," says another, "it is all in *one harmonious key.*" But what is a key of color? Is it made by all the values of one color, such as red, or by all the hues of equal value, such as the middle hues in our color solid?

(152) Certainly it is neither, for the rug has both light and dark colors; and, of the reds, yellows, greens, and blues, some are stronger and others weaker. Then what do we mean by a key of color? One must either continue to flounder about or frankly confess ignorance.

(153) Musical harmony explains itself in clear language. It 87 is illustrated by fixed and definite sound intervals, whose measured relations form the basis of musical composition. Each key has an unmistakable character, and the written score presents a statement that means practically the same thing to every person of musical intelligence. But the adequate terms of color harmony are yet to be worked out.

Let us leave these musical analogies, retaining only the clue that *a measured and orderly relation underlies the idea of harmony.* The color solid which has been the subject of these pages is built upon measured color relations. It unites measured scales of hue, value, and chroma, and gives a definite color name to every sensation from the maxima of color-light and color-strength to their disappearance in darkness.

(154) Must not this theoretical color solid, therefore, locate all the elements which combine to produce color harmony or color discord?32

(155) Instead of theorizing, let us experiment. As a child at the piano, who first strikes random and widely separated notes, but soon seeks for the intervals of a familiar air, so let us, after roaming over the color globe and its charts, select one familiar color, and study what others will combine with it to please the eye.

(156) Here is a grayish green stuff for a dress, and the little girl who is to wear it asks what other colors she may use with it. First let us find it on our instrument, so as to realize its relation to other degrees of color. Its value is 6,—one step above the equator of middle value. Its hue is green, G, and its chroma5. It is written $G^{6}/_{5}$.

(157) Color paths lead out from this point in every direction. 88 Where shall we find harmonious colors, where discordant, where those paths most frequently travelled? Are there new ones still to be explored?

(158)*There are three typical paths: one vertical,* with rapid change of value; *another lateral,* with rapid change of hue; and a *third inward,* through the neutral centre to seek the opposite color field. All other paths are combinations of two or three of these typical directions in the color solid.

Three typical color paths.

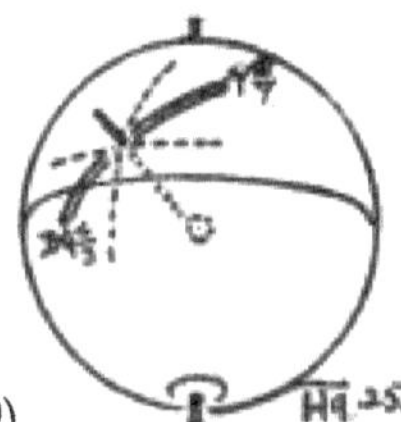

(159) 1. The vertical path finds only lighter and darker values of gray-green,—"self-colors or shades," they are generally called,—and offers a safe path, even for those deficient in color sensation, avoiding all complications of hue, and leaving the eye free to estimate different degrees of a single quality,—color-light.

(160) 2. The lateral path passes through neighboring hues on either side. In this case it is a sequence from blue, through green into yellow. This is simply change of hue, without change of value or chroma if the path be level, but, by inclining it, one end of the se-

quence becomes lighter, while the other end darkens. It thus becomes an intermediate between the first and second typical paths, combining, at each step, achange of hue with a change of value. This is more complicated, but also more interesting, showing how the character of the gray-green dress will be set off by a *lighter* hat of Leghorn straw, and further improved by a trimming of *darker* blue-green. The sequence can be made still more subtle and attractive by choosing a straw whose yellow is *stronger* than the green of the dress, while a *weaker*89 chroma of blue-green is used in the trimming. This is clearly expressed by the notation thus: $Y^{8}/7$, $G^{6}/5$, $BG^{4}/3$, and written on the score by three dots and their chromas,—7, 5, and 3 (see Fig.23).

(161) 3. The inward path which leads by increase of gray to the neutral centre, and on to the opposite hue red-purple, $RP^{4}/5$, is full of pitfalls for the inexpert. It combines great change of hue and chroma, with small change of value.

(162) If any other color point be chosen in place of gray-green, the same typical paths are just as easily traced, written by the notation, and recorded on the color score.

These paths trace sequences from any point in the color solid.

(163) In the construction of the color solid we saw that its scales were made of equal steps in hue, value, and chroma, and tested by balance on the centre of neutral gray. Any step will serve as a point of departure to trace regular sequences of the three types. The vertical type is a sequence of value only. It is somewhat tame, lacking the change of hue and chroma, but giving a monotonous harmony of regular values. The horizontal type traces a sequence of neighboring hues, less tame than the vertical type, but monotonous in value and chroma. The inward type connects opposite hues by a sequence of chroma balanced on middle gray, and is more stimulating to the eyes.

(164) These paths have so far been treated as made up of equal steps in each direction, with the accompanying idea of equal quantities of color at each step. But by using *unequal quantities of color*, the balance may be preserved by compensations to the intervals that separate the colors (see paragraphs 109, 110).

Unequal color quantities compensated by relations of hue, value, and chroma.

(165) Small bits of powerful color can be used to balance large 90
fields of weak chroma. For instance, aspot of strong reddish purple is balanced and enhanced by a field of gray-green. So an amethyst pin at the neck of the girl's dress will appear to advantage with the gown, and also with the Leghorn straw. But a large field of strong color, such as a cloth jacket of reddish purple, would be fatal to the measured harmony we seek.

(166) This use of a small point of strong chroma, if repeated at intervals, sets up a notion of rhythm; but, in order to be rhythmic, there must be recurrent emphasis, "asuccession of similar units, combining unlike elements." This quality must not be confused with the unaccented succession, seen in a measured scale of hue, value, or chroma.

Paper masks to isolate color intervals.

(167) A sheet of paper large enough to hide the color sphere may be perforated with three or more openings in a straight line, and applied against the surface, so as to isolate the steps of any sequence which we wish to study. Thus the sequence given in paragraph 160—$Y^{8}/_{7}$, $G^{6}/_{5}$, $BG^{4}/_{3}$—may be changed to bring it on the surface of the sphere, when it reads $Y^{8}/_{3}$, $G^{6}/_{5}$, $BG^{5}/_{5}$. Amask with round holes, spaced so as to uncover these three spots, relieves the eye from the distraction of other colors. Keeping the centre spot on green, the mask may be moved so as to study the effect of changing hue or value of the other two steps in the sequence.

(168) The sequence is lightened by sliding the whole mask upward, and darkened by dropping it lower. Then the result of using the same intervals in another field is easily studied by moving the mask to another part of the solid.

(169) Change of interval immediately modifies the character of a color sequence. This is readily shown by having an under-mask, with a long, continuous slit, and an over-mask whose perforations
91 are arranged in several rows, each row giving different spaces between the perforations. In the case of the girl's clothing, the same sequence produces quite a different effect, if two perforations of the

over-mask are brought nearer to select a lighter yellow-green dress, while the ends of the sequence remain unchanged. To move the middle perforation near the other end, selects a darker bluish green dress, on which the trimming will be less contrasted, while the hat appears brighter than before, because of greater contrast.

(170) The variations of color sequence which can thus be studied out by simple masks are almost endless; yet upon a measured system the character of each effect is easily described, and, if need be, preserved by a written record.

Invention of color groups.

(171) Experiments with variable masks for the selection of color intervals, such as have been described, soon stimulate the imagination, so that it conceives sequences through any part of the color solid. The color image becomes a permanent mental adjunct. Five middle colors, tempered with white and black, permit us to devise the greatest variety of sequences, some light, others dark, some combining small difference of chroma with large difference of hue, others uniting large intervals of chroma with small intervals of hue, and so on through a well-nigh inexhaustible series.

(172) As this constructive imagination gains power, the solid and its charts may be laid aside. *We can now think color consecutively.* Each color suggests its place in the system, and may be taken as a point of departure for the invention of groups to carry out a desired relation.

(173) This selective mental process is helped by the score described 92 in the last chapter; and the quantity of each color chosen for the group is easily indicated by a variable circle, drawn round the various points on the diagram. Thus, in the case of the child's clothes, alarge circle around $G^6/_5$ gives the area of that color as compared with smaller circles around $Y^8/_7$ and $BG^4/_3$, representing the area of the straw and the trimming.

(174) When the plotting of color groups has become instinctive from long practice, it opens a wide field of color study. Take as illustration the wings of butterflies or the many varieties of pansies. These fascinating color schemes can be written with indications of area that record their differences by a simple diagram. In the same

way, rugs, tapestries, mosaics,—whatever attracts by its beauty and harmony of color,—can be recorded and studied in measured terms; and the mental process of estimating hues, values, chromas, and areas by established scales must lead the color sense to finer and finer perceptions.

The same process serves as well to record the most annoying and inharmonious color groups. When sufficient of these records have been obtained, they furnish definite material for a contrast of the color combinations which please, with those that cause disgust. Such a contrast should discover some broad law of color harmony. It will then be in measured terms which can be clearly given; not a vague personal statement, conveying different meanings to each one who hearsit.

Constant exercise needed to train the color sense.

(175) Appreciation of beautiful color grows by exercise and discrimination, just as naturally as fine perception of music or literature. Each is an outlet for the expression of taste,—a language which may be used clumsily or with skill.

(176) As color perception becomes finer, it discards the more 93
crude and violent contrasts. Achild revels in strong chromas, but the mark of a colorist is ability to employ low chroma without impoverishing the color effect. As a boy's shrieks and groans can be tempered to musical utterance, so his debauches in violent red, green, and purple must be replaced by tempered hues.

(177) Raphael, Titian, Velasquez, Corot, Chavannes, and Whistler are masters in the use of gray. Personal bias may lead one colorist a little more toward warm colors, and another slightly toward the cool field, in each case attaining a sense of harmonious balance by tempered degrees of value and chroma.[33]

(178) It is not claimed that discipline in the use of subtle colors will make another Corot or Velasquez, but it will make for comprehension of their skill. It is grotesque to watch gaudily dressed persons going into ecstasies over the delicate coloring of a Botticelli, when the internal as well as the external evidence is against them.

(179) The colors which we choose, not only in personal apparel, but in our rooms and decorations, are mute witnesses to a stage of color perception.

If that perception is trained to finer distinctions, the mind can no longer be content with coarse expression. It begins to feel an incongruity between the "loud" color of the wall paper, bought because it was fashionable, and the quiet hues of the rug, which was a gift from some artistic friend. It sees that, although the furniture is covered with durable and costly materials, their color "swears" at that of the curtains and wood-work. In short, the 94 room has been jumbled together at various periods, without any plan or sense of color design.

(180) Good taste demands that a room be furnished, not alone for convenience and comfort, but also with an eye to the beauty of the various objects, so that, instead of confusing and destroying the colors, each may enhance the other. And, when this sense of color harmony is aroused, it selects and arranges the books, the rugs, the lamp shade, the souvenirs of travel and friendship, the wall paper, pictures, and hangings, so that they fit into a color scheme, not only charming to the eye at first glance, but which continues to please the mind as it traces out an intelligent plan, bringing all into general harmony.

(181) Nor will this cease when one room has been put to rights. Such a coloristic attitude is not satisfied until the vista into the next apartment is made attractive. Or should there be a suite of rooms, it demands that, with variety in each one, they all be brought into harmonious sequence. Thus the study of color finds immediate and practical use in daily life. It is a needed discipline of color vision, in the sense that geometry is a discipline of the mind, and it also enters into the pleasure and refinement of life at every step. Skill or awkwardness in its use exerts as positive an influence upon us as do the harmonies and discords of sound, and a far more continuous one. It is thought a defect to be unmusical. Should it not be considered a mark of defective cultivation to be insensitive to color?

(182) In this slight sketch of color education it has been assumed that we are to deal with those who have normal perceptions. But

there are some who inherit or develop various degrees of color-blindness; and a word in their behalf may be opportune.

(183) A case of total color-blindness is very rare, but a few 95 are on record. When a child shows deficient color perception,34 alittle care may save him much discomfort, and patient training may correct it. If he mismatches some hues, confuses their names, seems incapable of the finer distinctions of color, study to find the hues which he estimates well, and then help him to venture a little into that field where his perception is at fault. Improvement is pretty sure to follow when this is sympathetically done. One student, who never outgrew the habit of giving a purplish hue to all his work, despite many expedients and the use of various lights and colored objects to correct it, is the single exception among hundreds whom it has been my privilege to watch as they improved their first crude estimates, and gained skill in expressing their sense of Nature's subtle color.

(184) To sum up, the first chapter suggests a measured color system in place of guess-work. The next describes the three color qualities, and sketches a child's growth in color perception. The third tells how colors may be mingled in such proportions as to balance. After the impracticability of using spectral color has been shown in the fourth chapter, the fifth proceeds to build a practical color solid. The sixth provides for a written record of color, and the last applies all that has preceded to suggestions for the study of color harmony.

(185) Wide gaps appear in this outline. There is much that deserves fuller treatment. But, if the search for refined color and a clearer outlook upon its relations are stimulated by this fragmentary sketch, some of its faults may be overlooked.

32. Professor James says there are three classic stages in the career of a theory: "First, it is attacked as absurd; then admitted to be true, but obvious and insignificant; finally it is seen to be so important that its adversaries claim to be its discoverers."

33. "Nature's most lively hues are bathed in lilac grays. Spread all about us, yet visible only to the fine perception of the colorist, is this gray quality by which he appeals. Not he whose pictures abound in '*couleurs voyantes*,' but he who preserves in his work all the '*gris colorés*' is the good colorist."

Translation from J. F. Rafaelli, in *Annales Politiques & Litteraires.*

34. See Color Blindness in Glossary.

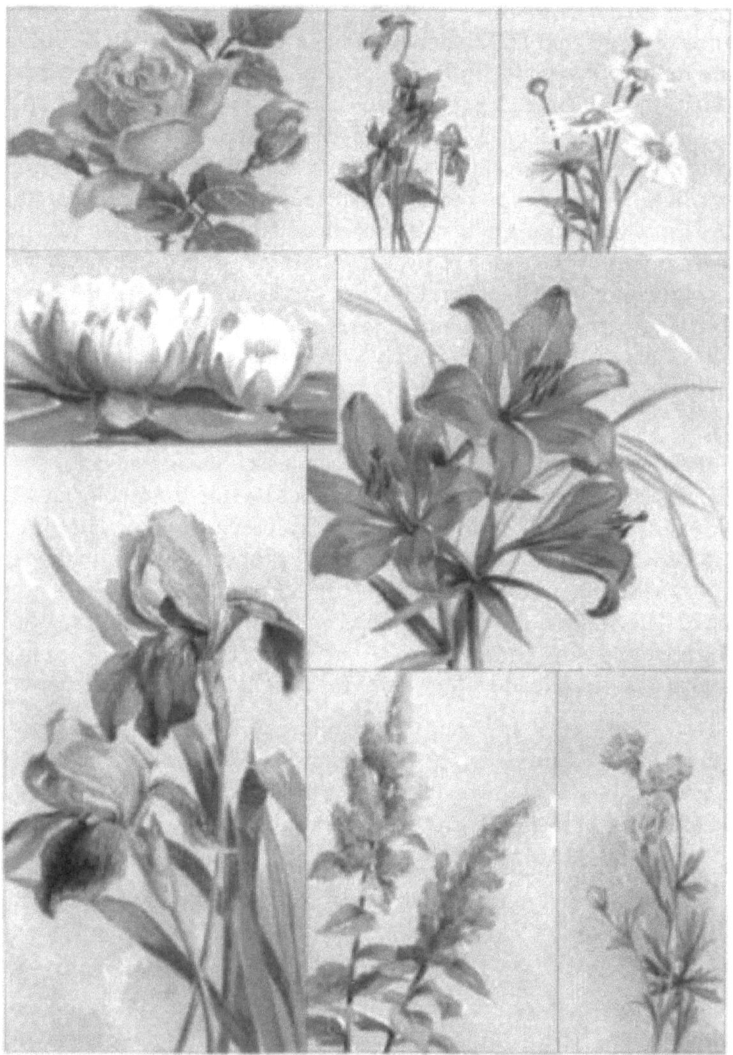

REPRODUCTION OF FLOWER STUDIES,
PAINTED WITH MUNSELL WATER COLOR

PUBLISHED BY
WADSWORTH, HOWLAND & CO., INCORPORATED, BOSTON, MASS.
97

PART II.

A COLOR SYSTEM AND COURSE OF STUDY BASED ON THE COLOR SOLID AND ITS CHARTS.

Arranged for nine years of school life.

GLOSSARY OF COLOR TERMS.

Taken from the Century Dictionary.

INDEX

(by paragraphs).

99

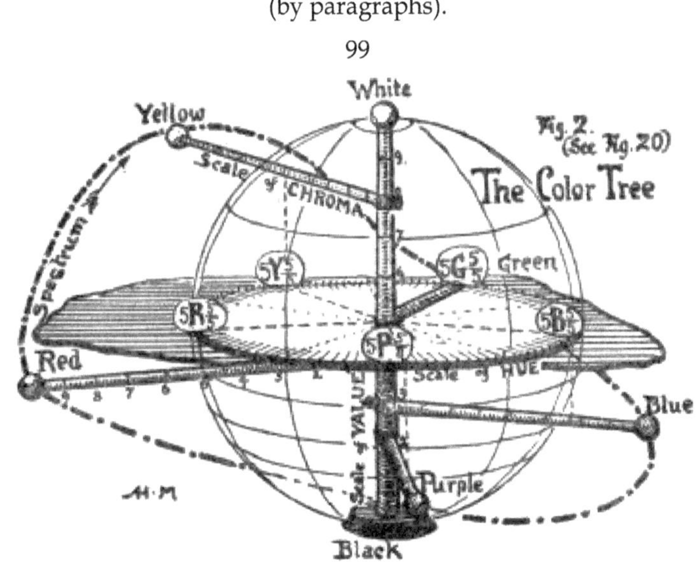

A COLOR SYSTEM WITH COURSE OF STUDY BASED ON THE COLOR SOLID AND ITS CHARTS

See Chapter II.

A COLOR SYSTEM AND COURSE OF STUDY BASED ON THE COLOR SOLID AND ITS CHARTS, ADAPTED TO NINE YEARS OF SCHOOL LIFE.

e.	**Subject.**	**Colors Studied.**	**Illustration.**	**Application.**	**Mate**
	HUES of color.	Red. R. Yellow. Y. Green. G. Blue. B. Purple. P.	Sought in Nature and Art.	Borders and Rosettes.	Colo crayc and p pers.
	HUES of color.	Yellow-red. YR. Green-yellow. GY. Blue-green. BG. Purple-blue. PB. Red-purple. RP.	Sought in Nature and Art.	Borders and Rosettes.	Colo crayc and p pers.

VALUES of color.	Light, middle, and dark R. " " " Y. " " " G. " " " B. " " " P.	Sought in Nature and Art.	Design.	Colo sphe
VALUES of color.	5 values of YR. ^{9}/, ^{7}/, ^{5}/, ^{3}/,^{1}/. " " " " GY. " " " " BG. " " " " PB. " " " " RP.	Sought in Nature and Art.	Design.	Char
CHROMAS of color.	3 chromas of R^5/. " " " Y^5/. " " " G^5/. " " " B^5/. " " " P^5/.	Sought in Nature and Art.	Design.	Char
CHROMAS of color.	3 chromas of YR^5/. " " " GY^5/. " " " BG^5/. " " " PB^5/. " " " RP^5/. " " " R^7/ and R^3/. " " " Y^7/ "	Sought in Nature and Art.	Design.	Colo Tree

Y3/.
„„ „G7/ „
G3/.
„„ „B7/ „
B3/.
„„ „P7/ „
P3/.

To OBSERVE IMITATE & WRITE	color by HUE, VALUE, and CHROMA	"	"	Paint

QUANTITY of color.

Pairs of equal area and unequal area Balanced by HUE, VALUE, and CHROMA. " Paint

QUANTITY of color.

Triads of equal area and unequal area Balanced by HUE, VALUE, and CHROMA. " Paint

101

STUDY OF SINGLE HUES AND THEIR SEQUENCE. Two Years.

FIRST GRADE LESSONS.

1. Talk about familiar objects, to bring out color names, as toys,

flowers,

2. clothing, birds, insects, etc.

3. Show soap bubbles and prismatic spectrum.

4. Teach term HUE. Hues of flowers, spectrum, plumage of birds, etc.

5. Show MIDDLE35 RED. Find other reds.

6. „ YELLOW. „yellows, and compare with reds.

7. „ GREEN. „greens, „ „and yellows.

8. „ BLUE. „blues, „preceding hues.

9. „ PURPLE. „purples, „ „

10–15. Review FIVE MIDDLE HUES,35 match with colored papers, and place in circle.

16–20. Show COLOR SPHERE. Find sequence of five middle hues. Memorize order.

21. Middle red imitated with crayon, named and written by initialR.

22. „ yellow„ „ „ „ „Y.

23. „ green „ „ „ „ „G.

24. „ blue „ „ „ „ „B.

25. „ purple „ „ „ „ „P.

26–30. Review, using middle hues35 in borders and rosettes for design.

Aim.—To recognize sequence of five middle hues.
To name, match, imitate, write, and arrange them.

SECOND GRADE LESSONS.

1–3. Review sequence of five middle hues.35

4. Show a hue INTERMEDIATE between red and yellow. Find it in objects.

5. Compare with red and yellow.

6. Recognize and name YELLOW-RED. Match, imitate, and writeYR.

7–8. Show GREEN-YELLOW between Treat as above, and

green and yellow. writeGY.

9–10. „BLUE-GREEN „blue and green. 〃 〃 „BG.

11–12. „PURPLE-BLUE „purple and blue. 〃 〃 „PB.

13–14. „RED-PURPLE „red and purple. 〃 〃 „RP.

15–20. Make circle of ten hues. Place Intermediates, and memorize order so as to repeat forward or backward. Match, imitate, and write by initials.

21–25. Find sequence of ten hues on COLOR SPHERE. Compare with hues of natural objects.

26-30. Review, using any two hues in sequence for borders and rosettes.

Aim.—To recognize sequence of ten hues, made up of five middle35 hues and the five intermediates. To name, match, write, imitate, and arrange them.

102

STUDY OF SINGLE VALUES AND THEIR SEQUENCE. Two Years.

THIRD GRADE LESSONS.

1. Review sequence of ten hues.

2.

3. Recognize, name, match, imitate, write, and find them on the COLOR SPHERE. Also in objects.

4. Teach use of term VALUE. Color value recognized apart from color hue.

5. Find values of red, lighter and darker than the middle value already familiar.

7.	THREE VALUES of RED.	Find on sphere. Name as LIGHT, MIDDLE, and DARK values of red.
8.	"	Imitate with crayons, and write them as 3, 5, and7.
9.	„YELLOW.	Compare with above.
10.		Recognize, name, match, and imitate with crayons.
11.	„GREEN.	Compare, and treat as above.
12.		Find on sphere and in objects.
13.	„BLUE.	" "
14.		
15.	„PURPLE.	" "
16.		

17-20. Review, combining two values and a single hue for design.36

Aim.—To recognize a sequence combining three values and five middle hues.

To name, match, imitate, and arrange them.

FOURTH GRADE LESSONS.

1. Review sequence of three values in each of the five middle hues.

2. 3.		To recognize, name, match, imitate, and find them on sphere and in objects.	
4. 5.	Show FIVE VALUES of	RED. Find them on large color sphere. Number them 1, 3, 5, 7,9. Match, imitate, and write.	
6.	"	BLUE-GREEN.„ „ „	
7.	"	PURPLE-BLUE compared with Yellow.	Treat as above and review.
8.	"	RED-PURPLE „ Green.	
9.	"	YELLOW-RED „ Blue.	
10.	"	GREEN-YELLOW „ Purple.	

Aim.—To recognize sequences combining five values in each of ten hues.

To name, match, imitate, WRITE, and arrange them.

103

STUDY OF SINGLE CHROMAS AND THEIR SEQUENCES. Two Years.

FIFTH GRADE LESSONS.

1. Review sequences of hue and value. Find them on the color sphere. Name, match, imitate, write, and arrange them by hue and value.

2.	Teach use of term CHROMA.	Compare three chromas with three values of red. Name them WEAK, MIDDLE, and STRONG chromas. Find in nature and art.
3.	THREE CHROMAS of RED.	Compare with three of blue-green.
4.		Show COLOR TREE. Suggest unequal chroma of hues.
5.	„ YELLOW.	Compare with three chromas of purple-blue.
6.	„ GREEN	„ „ red-purple.
7.	„ BLUE.	„ „ yellow-red.
8.	„ PURPLE.	„ „ green-yellow.

9. Arrange five middle hues in circle, described as on the surface of the Color Sphere (middle chroma), with weaker chromas inside, and stronger chromas outside, the sphere.

10. Review,—to find these sequences of chroma in nature and art.

Aim.—To recognize sequences combining three chromas, middle value, and ten hues.
To name, match, imitate, and arrange them.

SIXTH GRADE LESSONS.

1. Review sequences combining three chromas, five hues, and middle value.

 Find on Color Tree, name, match, imitate, and arrange them.

2. THREE CHROMAS of LIGHTER and DARKER RED. Compare with middle red.
3. Write „ „ „ „ as a fraction, chroma under value, using 3, 5, and7. Thus R5/7.
4. Find „ „ RED, and compare with darker blue-green.
5. THREE CHROMAS of LIGHTER and DARKER YELLOW, with purple-blue.
6. „ „ „ „GREEN, „red-purple.
7. „ „ „ „BLUE, „yellow-red.
8. „ „ „ „PURPLE, „green-yellow.
9. Colors in nature and art, defined by hue, value, and chroma. Named, matched, imitated, written, and arranged by Color Sphere and Tree.
10. Review,—to find sequences combining three chromas, five values, and ten hues.

Aim.—To recognize sequences of chroma, as separate from sequences of hue or sequences of value.
To name, match, write, imitate, and arrange colors in terms of their hue, value, and chroma.

104

COLOR EXPRESSION IN TERMS OF THE HUES, VALUES, AND CHROMAS.

SEVENTH GRADE LESSONS.

1. Review sequences of hue (initial), value (upper numeral), & chroma (lower numeral).
2. „ „ „ „
3. Exercises in expressing colors of natural objects by the NOTATION, and
4. tracing their relation by the spherical solid.
5. REDS in Nature and Art, imitated, written, and traced „
6. YELLOWS„ „ „ „
7. GREENS„ „ „ „
8. BLUES „ „ „ „
9. PURPLES„ „ „ „
10. ONE COLOR PAIR selected, defined, and arranged for design. (See note 4th Grade.)

Aim.—To define any color by its hue, value, and chroma.
To imitate with pigments and writeit.

EIGHTH GRADE LESSONS.

1. Review sequences, and select colors which balance. Illustrate the term.
2. BALANCE of light and dark,—weak and strong,—hot and cold colors.
3. RED and blue-green balanced in hue, value, and chroma, with EQUAL AREAS.
4. YELLOW „ purple-blue „ „
5. GREEN „ red-purple „ „
6. BLUE „ yellow-red „ „
7. PURPLE „ green-yellow „ „
8. UNEQUAL AREAS of the above pairs balanced by compensating

9. qualities of hue, value, and chroma. Examples from nature and art.

10. ONE COLOR PAIR of unequal areas selected, defined, and used in design.

Aim.—To BALANCE colors by area, hue, value, and chroma. To imitate with pigments and write the balance by the notation.

NINTH GRADE LESSONS.

1. Review balance of color pairs, by area, hue, value, and chroma.
2. To recognize, name, imitate, write, and record them.
3. SELECTION of two colors to balance a given RED.
4. " " "" YELLOW.
5. " " "" GREEN.
6. " " "" BLUE.
7. " " "" PURPLE.
8–10. TRIAD of color, selected, balanced, written, and used in design.

Aim.—To recognize triple balance of color, and express it in terms of area, hue, value, and chroma. Also to use it in design.

35. The term MIDDLE, as used in this course of color study, is understood to mean only the five principal hues which stand midway in the scales of VALUE and CHROMA. Strictly speaking, their five intermediates are also midway of the scales; but they are obtained by mixture of the five principal hues, as shown in their names, and are of secondary importance.

Footnote 35 is referenced five times in the first two years' lessons.

36. These ten lessons in this and succeeding grades are devoted to color perception only. Their application to design is a part of the general course in drawing, and will be so considered in the succeeding grades. Note that, although thus far nothing has been said about complementary hues, the child has been led to associate them in opposite pairs by the color sphere. (See Chapter III., p.76.)

GLOSSARY OF COLOR TERMS

TAKEN FROM
THE

CENTURY DICTIONARY.

107

GLOSSARY

The color definitions here employed are taken from the Century Dictionary. Special attention is called to the cross references which serve to differentiate HUE, VALUE, and CHROMA.

AFTER IMAGE.—An image perceived after withdrawing the eye from a brilliantly illuminated object. Such images are called positive when their colors are the same as that of the object, and negative when they are its complementary colors.

BLUE.—Of the color of the clear sky; of the color of the spectrum between wave lengths .505 and .415 micron, and more especially .487 and .460; or of such light mixed with white; azure, cerulean.

BLACK.—Possessing in the highest degree the property of absorbing light; reflecting and transmitting little or no light; of the color of soot or coal; of the darkest possible hue; sable. Optically, wholly destitute of color, or absolutely dark, whether from the absence or the total absorption of light. Opposed to white.

BROWN.—A dark color, inclined to red or yellow, obtained by mixing red, black, and yellow.

CHROMA.—The degree of departure of a color sensation from that of white or gray; the intensity of distinctive hue; color intensity.

CHROMATIC.—Relating to or of the nature of color.

COBALT BLUE.—A pure blue tending toward cyan blue and of high luminosity; also called Hungary blue, Lethner's blue, and Paris blue.

108

COLOR.—Objectively, that quality of a thing or appearance which is perceived by the eye alone, independently of the form of the thing; subjectively, asensation peculiar to the organ of vision, and arising from the optic nerve.

COLOR BLINDNESS.—Incapacity for perceiving colors, independent of the capacity for distinguishing light and shade. The most common form is inability to perceive red as a distinct color, red objects being confounded with gray or green; and next in frequency is the inability to perceive green.

COLOR CONSTANTS.—The numbers which measure the quantities, as well as any other system of three numbers for defining colors, are called constants of color.

COLOR VARIABLES.—Colors vary in CHROMA, or freedom from admixture of white light; in BRIGHTNESS, or luminosity; and in HUE, which roughly corresponds to the mean wave length of the light emitted.

COLORS, COMPLEMENTARY.—Those pairs of color which when mixed produce white or gray light, such as red and green-blue, yellow and indigo-blue, green-yellow and violet.

COLORS, PRIMARY.—The red, green, and violet light of the spectrum, from the mixture of which all other colors can be produced. Also called fundamental colors.

DYESTUFFS.—In commerce, any dyewood, lichen, or dyecake used in dyeing and staining.

ELECTRIC LIGHT.—Light produced by electricity and of two general kinds, the arc light and the incandescent light. In the first the voltaic arc is employed. In the second a resisting conductor is rendered incandescent by the current.

ENAMEL.—In the fine arts a vitreous substance or glass, opaque or transparent, and variously colored, applied as a coating on a surface of metal or of porcelain.

109

GRATING, DIFFRACTION.—A series of fine parallel lines on a surface of glass, or polished metal, ruled very close together, at the rate of 10,000 to 20,000 or even 40,000 to the inch; distinctively called a diffraction or a diffraction grating, much used in spectroscopic work.

GRAY.—A color having little or no distinctive hue (CHROMA) and only moderate luminosity.

GREEN.—The color of ordinary foliage; the color seen in the solar spectrum between wave lengths 0.511 and 0.543 micron.

EMERALD GREEN.—A highly chromatic and extraordinarily luminous green of the color of the spectrum at wave length 0.524 micron. It recalls the emerald by its brilliancy, but not by its tint; applied generally to the aceto-arsenate of copper. Usually known as Paris green.

HIGH COLOR.—A hue which excites intensely chromatic color sensations.

HUE.—Specifically and technically, distinctive quality of coloring in an object or on a surface; the respect in which red, yellow, green, blue, etc., differ one from another; that in which colors of equal luminosity and CHROMA may differ.

INDIGO.—The violet-blue color of the spectrum, extending, according to Helmholtz, from G two-thirds of the way to F in the prismatic spectrum. The name was introduced by Newton, but has lately been discarded by the best writers.

LIGHT.—Adjective applied to colors highly luminous and more or less deficient in CHROMA.

LUMINOSITY.—Specifically, the intensity of light in a color, measured photometrically; that is to say, astandard light has its intensity, or *vis viva,* altered, until it produces the impression of being equally bright with the color whose light is to be 110 determined; and the measure of the *vis viva* of the altered light, relatively to its standard intensity, is then taken as the luminosity of the color in question.

MAXWELL COLOR DISCS.—Discs having each a single color, and slit radially so that one may be made to lap over another to any desired extent. By rotating these on a spindle, the effect of combining certain colors in varying proportions can be studied.

MICRON.—The millionth part of a metre, or 1/23400 of an English inch. The term has been formally adopted by the International

Commission of Weights and Measures, representing the civilized nations of the world, and is adopted by all metrologists.

ORANGE.—A reddish yellow color, of which the orange is the type.

VISION, PERSISTENCE OF.—The continuance of a visual impression upon the retina of the eye after the exciting cause is removed. The length of time varies with the intensity of the light and the excitability of the retina, and ordinarily is brief, though the duration may be for hours, or even days. The after image may be either positive or negative, the latter when the bright part appears dark and the colored parts in their corresponding contrast colors. It is because of this persistence that, for example, afirebrand moved very rapidly appears as a band or circle of light.

PHOTOMETER.—An instrument used to measure the intensity of light. Specifically, to compare the relative intensities of the light emitted from various sources.

PIGMENT.—Any substance that is or can be used by painters to impart color to bodies.

PINK.—A red color of low chroma, but high luminosity, inclining toward purple.

111

PRIMARY COLORS.—See Colors, primary.

PURE COLOR.—A color produced by homogeneous light. Any very brilliant or decided color.

PURPLE.—A color formed by the mixture of blue and red, including the violet of the spectrum above wave length 0.417, which is nearly a violet blue, and extending to, but not including, crimson.

RAINBOW.—A bow or an arc of a circle, consisting of the prismatic colors, formed by the refraction and the reflection of rays of light from drops of rain or vapor, appearing in the part of the heavens opposite to the sun.

RED.—A color more or less resembling that of blood, or the lower end of the spectrum. Red is one of the most general color names, and embraces colors ranging in hue from aniline to scarlet iodide of mercury and red lead. Ared yellower than vermilion is called scarlet. One much more crimson is called crimson red. Avery dark red, if pure or crimson, is called maroon; if brownish, chestnut or chocolate. Apale red—that is, one of low CHROMA and high LUMINOSITY—is called a pink, ranging from rose pink or pale crimson to salmon pink or pale scarlet.

VENETIAN RED.—An important pigment used by artists, somewhat darker than brick red in color, and very permanent.

RETINA.—The innermost and chiefly nervous coat of the posterior part of the eyeball.

SATURATION, OF COLORS.—In optics the degree of admixture with white, the saturation diminishing as the amount of white is increased. In other words, the highest degree of saturation belongs to a given color when in the state of greatest purity.

112

SCALE.—A graded system, by reference to which the degree, intensity, or quality of a sense perception may be estimated.

SHADE.—Degree or gradation of defective luminosity in a color, often used vaguely from the fact that paleness, or high luminosity, combined with defective CHROMA, is confounded with high luminosity by itself. See Color, Hue, and Tint.

SPECTRUM.—In physics the continuous band of light showing the successive prismatic colors, or the isolated lines or bands of color, observed when the radiation from such a source as the sun or an ignited vapor in a gas flame is viewed after having been passed through a prism (prismatic spectrum) or reflected from a diffraction grating (diffraction or interference spectrum). See Rainbow.

TINT.—A variety of color; especially and properly, aluminous variety of low CHROMA; also, abstractly, the respect in which a color may be raised by more or less admixture of white, which at once increases the luminosity and diminishes the CHROMA.

TONE.—A sound having definiteness and continuity enough so that its pitch, force, and quality may be readily estimated by the ear. Musical sound opposed to noise. The prevailing effect of a color.

Ultramarine.—A beautiful natural blue pigment, obtained from the mineral lapis-lazuli.

VALUE.—In painting and the allied arts, relation of one object, part, or atmospheric plane of a picture to the others, with reference to light and shade, the idea of HUE being abstracted.

Vermilion.—The red sulphate of mercury.

Violet.—A general class of colors, of which the violet flower is a 113 highly chromatic example. The sensation is produced by a pure blue whose CHROMA has been diminished while its LUMINOSITY has been increased. Thus blue and violet are the same color, though the sensations are different. Amere increase of illumination may cause a violet blue to appear violet, with a diminution of apparent CHROMA. This color, called violet or blue according to the quality of the sensation it excites, is one of the three fundamental colors of Young's theory. Adeep blue tinged with red.

Viridian.—Same as Veronese green.

White.—A color transmitting, and so reflecting to the eye, all the rays of the spectrum, combined in the same proportion as in the impinging light.

Yellow.—The color of gold and of light, of wave length 0.581 micron. The name is restricted to highly chromatic and luminous colors. When reduced in CHROMA, it becomes buff; when reduced in LUMINOSITY, acool brown. See Brown.

Veronese Green.—A pigment consisting of hydrated chromium sesquioxide. It is a clear bluish green of great permanency. Also called Viridian.

114

INDEX BY PARAGRAPHS.

The MUNSELL PHOTOMETER

Patented November 19, 1901

A portable, daylight instrument, adapted to laboratory work in general, and of especial service in the comparison of color values. Placed in the course of Optical Measurements at the Massachusetts Institute of Technology

Price, $50

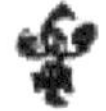

IN PREPARATION

A COLOR ATLAS

Also text-books and models specially designed to serve in the education of the color sense

For comparison purposes, here is the Color Balance illustration (Appendix III) using the colors of your computer monitor (red, green, blue):

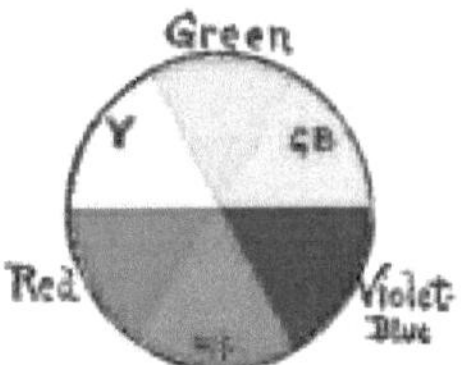

The three "secondary" colors each combine two of the three colors in equal amounts. These are the colors used by your printer: yellow, cyan (blue + green) and magenta (red + blue).